Witnessing to the Fire

**Spiritual Direction and the Development of Directors,
One Center's Experience**

*Madeline Birmingham
and William J. Connolly*

Sheed & Ward

Chapter 6 is a revised version of an article that appeared in
Human Development, Vol. 8, No. 1, Spring 1987.

Hartford, CT: Jesuit Educational Center for Human Development.
(In 1987 Cambridge, MA)

Scripture quotations are taken from the Revised English Bible.
Oxford and Cambridge. University Presses, 1989.

Sheed & Ward™ is a service of The National Catholic Reporter
Publishing Company.

◆

Library of Congress Cataloguing-in-Publication Data

Birmingham, Madeline.
    Witnessing to the fire : spiritual direction and the develop-
ment of directors, one center's experience / Madeline Birmingham
and William J. Connolly.
       p.   cm.
    ISBN: 1-55612-666-2 (alk. paper)
    1. Spiritual direction. 2. Center for Religious Development
(Cambridge, Mass.) I. Connolly, William J. II. Title.
BX2350.7.B45 1993
253.5'3—dc20   93-27071
                                            CIP

◆

Published by: Sheed & Ward
                115 E. Armour Blvd.
                P.O. Box 419492
                Kansas City, MO 64141-6492

To order, call: (800) 333-7373

Contents

For John and Margaret Coady,
faithful friends

Acknowledgements

When you take 10 years to write a book, you end up with more debts than you can repay. You may not even have the space to acknowledge them all. But let us try.

Before all else, we give thanks to the Mystery of God who, undeterred by human fumbling, casts fire on our earth.

Next there is the fundamental debt we owe to those who have come to the Center for direction. It is they who have consistently shown us the fire we have tried to reflect in this book.

We recall with more appreciation than we have words to convey those colleagues who, as full-time staff, have been responsible for the Center's ministry. Some initiated it; some continued it; all took part in developing it. We hope they will find our discussion not totally unworthy of their contribution. They are William A. Barry, Robert G. Doherty, Robert E. Lindsay, Daniel J. Lusch, Joseph F. MacFarlane, Joseph E. McCormick, Anne Harvey, Paul T. Lucey, Francine Zeller, James M. Keegan, Michael Mohally, J. Thomas Hamel, and Kenneth J. Hughes.

We thank the associates who have joined us each year since 1972 and have worked with us as spiritual directors. They have made it possible for a numerous succession of those who came for direction to become more aware of the fire.

We are grateful for the approval, help, and support given to the Center's ministry by the successive Jesuit provincial administrations that have been responsible for it. The present provincial, Bill Barry, was director of the Center in its first years.

Because the deeds of provincial administrators may readily be forgotten, we recall in particular William G. Guindon, provincial when the Center was established. The vision and initiative he showed in suggesting the possibility of a Center, welcoming the unusual project proposed to him, and giving his authorization, were both characteristic of him and deserving of our deepest appreciation.

Several part-time staff members have led the associates to new levels of reflection on their ministry. Drawing from their specialized background in theology or psychology, they have provided the associates with insightful presentations and encouraged them to vigorous discussion. They are Brien O. McDermott, James J. Gill, Nancy Ring, and William E. Reiser.

Bill Barry, David Donovan, Thomas Gallagher and James Keegan have generously shared their expertise at group work meetings. David Donovan and Jim Keegan, before he joined the full-time staff, served as part-time supervisors.

Those who assisted the associates as facilitators at group dynamics sessions until 1980, and those who have assisted both associates and staff at group life since then have performed a difficult and valuable task. We thank them for the service they rendered us and the generosity with which they performed it. They are Anne Harvey, Kathleen Murphy, Gerald J. Calhoun, Kathy Galvin, Bill Burritt, Patricia Johnson, and Richard M. O'Brien.

Since the early 1980s, the Center has benefited from the unfailing interest and expertise of an advisory board. Its members have assisted the staff with administrative issues, contributed to planning for the future, and shared in both our worries and our achievements. The board members, past and present: Janet Eisner, H. Francis Cluff, Richard Friedrichs, Brian O. McDermott, Clyde Evans, William Kremmell, and Catherine Hannigan.

We owe a great debt, too, to four consultants who have helped the staff to resolve difficulties and keep a clear focus and a steady balance in their ministry. They are Gerald J. Calhoun, James J. Gill, James Muller, and Gerald G. Wyrwas.

The secretary-receptionist is the first to greet those who come to the Center. It is she who shows them the warmth which everyone at the Center wants to welcome them. This is a true ministerial service and we want to thank those who have offered it. They are Janet Marsocci, Evelyn Liberatore, Deborah Cole, Mary Ellen Johnson, Rita McCormick, Virginia Stanton, and Patricia T. Babish.

Beginning with Evelyn Liberatore, who worked with us in this position for 14 pioneering and memorable years, these women added to their other tasks the typing of the numerous drafts of this book. They, with Cindy Hill and Shannon McKenna, were responsible for bringing it gradually to the form in which it exists today.

Susan B. Walker gave us our first editorial assistance, and Tom Hamel added to his staff work the task of shepherding the typing through its final, crucial stage.

The book owes its existence in significant ways to Jim Gill, the editor of *Human Development*. Alert as he is to every opportunity to advance spiritual ministry, he was the first to recognize the potential value of a book that would describe and discuss the lengthy experience of one Center. It was his enthusiasm that persuaded us to envision it. He then chaired and recorded over two years the meetings in which, with Anne Harvey, at that time a member of the staff, we discussed the ideas from which this book developed. It was his probing interest that spurred us to shape our thought and clarify our focus. When the manuscript was finally completed, he and the *Human Development* staff found a publisher for it.

Preface

In the course of a convivial evening in 1971, one of the writers of this book confided to a companion that he and several associates were about to launch a new pastoral enterprise: a spiritual direction center. The venture was innovative. As far as the planners knew, nothing else of the kind existed. It had been planned in common by those who would staff it. Their hopes were multiple and ambitious, but their basic aim was simple: to assist people who wanted to let God develop a unique relationship with them and thought they would benefit from talking about it.

As he warmed to a favorite topic, the speaker noticed that his companion had fallen silent. Thinking that so novel an enterprise might not be comprehensible without further explanation, he forged ahead with his description until, abruptly, his companion blurted: "But who would come?"

Who would come? No one knew. A desire was abroad that might prompt people to respond to the new venture. As the companion of that faraway evening indicated, however, a skeptical assessment of the enterprise was not unreasonable.

Now, 20 years later, we can answer questions no one could answer then. We can also pass beyond the questions of that time to explore a ministry of spiritual direction that hardly existed then.

In this book we will describe and discuss the experience of the spiritual direction center spoken of that night. In our description we emphasize experience, not ideas. We do so in the hope that this description of one center's experience, despite its limited scope, will contribute to a continuing discussion of the spiritual direction ministry.

When we began work on the book in the early 1980s, we expected to complete it in two or three years. Now, a decade later, we realize that a satisfactory treatment of all aspects of the Center's experience is still beyond us. The nature of the Center is partly responsible for this. The Center for Religious Development, located in Cambridge, Massachusetts, though a modest establishment, has multiple purposes.

The Center has been engaged in the giving of spiritual direction since 1971; it has been committed to observing and writing about spiritual life and spiritual direction; and it has conducted numerous developmental programs designed to enable directors to meet more fully the demands of their ministry. Of these developmental programs, the one to which the staff has devoted most time and thought has been the nine-month associates' program conducted since 1972 at the Center itself.

The Center has also collaborated in programs sponsored by other institutions. Notable among these collaborative programs has been the concentration in spirituality and ministry offered by the Institute of Religious Education and Pastoral Ministry of Boston College. The concentration represents a pioneer endeavor aimed at enabling generalist pastoral ministers to help adults develop the spiritual dimension of their lives.

If we had given detailed attention to all the Center's activities, the book would be endowed with all the piquancy of a telephone directory. To avoid diffuseness, we have made a crucial choice. Rather than try to describe all the Center's endeavors, we decided to concentrate our attention on two: the giving of spiritual direction and the associates' program. Examining both permits us to discuss spiritual direction from complementary perspectives. Together they embody most of the key elements of the Center's ministry.

This choice gives focus to the book. Regrettably, it has prevented us from describing in detail other ventures that have also taught us much about the experience of direction.

We have been selective in other respects too. Though the range of subjects and issues that come under consideration in spiritual direction is as broad and varied as human experience itself, we have concentrated on the primary focus of direction, the relationship with God. We have not given the same attention to the psychological and social circumstances of the directee, important though these circumstances are. Whatever we could say about personality types, the Enneagram, addiction, and spiritual reading, for instance, has been said better by other writers. We hope that the straightforward attention we give to the dynamics of the developing relationship with God will complement their work.

Finally, we have been selective in the choice of a principal theme and a title for the book. Early in our writing, that theme proposed itself convincingly. The establishment and development of the Center were accomplished by a group of people who had agreed that only by observing, planning, and working together could they give their best efforts to the developing of a ministry they passionately believed in. The closeness of the cooperation that resulted and has been continued over the years deserves to be celebrated. It has been responsible for all the Center's initiatives and is a recurrent theme of this book.

Staff members at CRD have said over the years that God was showing that God wanted to do something there. Although the Center did not publicize its direction program, men and women from the most disparate backgrounds would appear at the door, asking for spiritual direction and ready to benefit from it. Elusive as financial support frequently proved, we usually had enough money at year's end to balance the budget. Most telling for us, however, was the consistency with which the able and engaged people who worked with us found God interacting with those who came to them for direction. This consistency became so noticeable in recent years that we have begun to say to new associates: "You may not have seen it yet, but you will."

As we write about what we believe is the action of God at the Center, we find ourselves subject to two different moods at variance with one another. One is exultation. We are delighted to have seen the fire God has cast upon the earth. The other is diffidence. We are afraid we will seem to be taking credit for God's action, or credit at least for having recognized God's action. We have decided to let exultation have its way.

The ministry of spiritual direction has shown astonishing vitality during the last two decades, both in the United States and in other countries. As we look back on the writing of this book, we recall the conversations we have had during those years with directors who worked in other places and in conditions different from ours. Those conversations have kept us aware that CRD is only one setting in which that vitality has appeared. We hope that our description and discussion will assist other groups and individuals engaged in this ministry to ponder their experience, as their experience has encouraged us to ponder ours.

We owe what we know about spiritual direction and most of what we know about spiritual life to those who have come to us for direction. What we know about the development of directors we have learned from directors themselves. Those who have come to us for direction have spoken to us in confidence, and directors have spoken to us in confidence too. We have respected their confidence and their right to privacy. In developing examples, we have been careful to express the truth of people's experience without compromising the commitment to confidentiality and privacy required by our ministry.

Aside from the preface and the conclusion, the book falls into four parts.

The first, consisting of chapters 1 and 2, introduces the reader to the Center. It describes the Center's origin and sketches its evolution. In the course of this description, attention is given to a number of salient attitudes that have come to characterize the Center's ministry. Among these attitudes, its approach to religious development is singled out for extensive discussion.

The second part—chapters 3 and 4—addresses the question: Who comes? It introduces the men and women who are primarily responsible for the spiritual direction that takes place at the Center: those who take direction there and those who give it. What brings them and how they come to participate are principal concerns of these chapters.

The third part, consisting of chapters 5, 6, and 7, describes and explores the three major components of the Center's ministry: the development of the faith-in-practice of the director, direction itself, and the developmental supervision of the director.

The final section—chapters 8 and 9—describes and discusses the associates' program as it is experienced by the associates and, in the final chapter, the spiritual journey experienced by those who come for direction. The final chapter is meant to be the culminating chapter. It is the experience of those who come for direction that witnesses most signally to the fire.

Chapter 1

The Center for Religious Development

The Center for Religious Development is both a place and an enterprise. The building, located on a busy thoroughfare in Cambridge, Massachusetts, is a handsome, elderly three-decker. It looks like what it was built to be: a substantial residence for middle-class families. It is a homey place.

The enterprise it now houses is as unpretentious as the building. This enterprise was established in the hope that it could contribute to the development of the ministry of spiritual direction, one of the least conspicuous of Christian ministries.

Spiritual direction is not the only activity that takes place at the Center, but it is the one all the other activities either serve or depend on. It is also the one to which most time is given. In the average week 100 to 150 people come to the Center for spiritual direction.

Since "spiritual direction" has acquired a wide variety of meanings, the reader will need a preliminary description of what we mean by the term before we proceed further with this chapter. Spiritual direction, we have just said, is the central activity that takes place at the Center. In much the same way the exploration and description of one's experience of God is the central activity of spiritual direction. Everything else that takes place at the Center, no matter how important it may be, is peripheral to the opportunity the Center gives people to talk about their experience of God.

To clarify, we would like to describe and comment on an incident that could occur in anyone's life.

A Man by the Sea

A man in his mid-40s sits on a cliff in Maine overlooking the North Atlantic. It is a radiant afternoon in June. He is a lawyer, and he has gone there to consider withdrawing from a long-standing partnership with a close friend whose heavy drinking is threatening to destroy their firm. He has come, then, with his mind filled with a painful problem. Shortly after his arrival on the cliff, however, he finds himself absorbed in studying the breakers as they advance, white manes flying, and gazing out at the limitless expanse of brilliant, blue-gray sea beyond them. Slowly, gradually, he begins to feel quiet and happy.

After some time he says to himself: "What I am seeing is telling me something about what God is like." A few minutes later he adds: "It is also telling me something about what I am like—the wonder that may always be there in me but that I am seldom aware of." As the afternoon wears on he says: "I'd like to tell someone about this."

The experience of gazing, becoming aware, and reacting has now come to a close. It was not a spectacular experience. As we have said, it could happen to anyone. But he continues to think about it. It has given him relief from the anxiety about his firm that he usually experiences when he is not busy. He has not forgotten the problem he came to consider, but his anxiety has diminished. He finds himself feeling more relaxed and confident. Something about this experience has come close to his core. He does not want to analyze the experience. He would, however, like to remain attentive to what it has told him.

What Happened?

If you knew him and came upon him just then, you might say: "You were completely engrossed. What was so interesting?" He might reply that he liked gazing at the sea, that he liked what he saw there. If he knew you well, he might add that he is not usually that sensitive to nature. He might pause then, and after a moment say that he wished he could say more, but he did not have the words for it.

Suppose you now reread this man's experience and ask yourself: "What happened?" Different readers will perceive the experience differently. One might say, "He was musing by the ocean and forgot his troubles for a while." Another: "The ocean had a calming effect on him." Yet another: "He thought of God."

All these comments would be true to the experience as we have described it, and the man's own comments also reflect it accurately. But more happened that neither the readers we have quoted nor the man himself has mentioned. Looking at the breakers and the sea made him feel quiet and happy. What he saw said something to him about what God is like. It said something, too, about a wonder in himself. What he saw also made him want to tell someone about it.

Talking About What Happened

This impulse to tell someone about moving experiences that have to do with God is quite common. There are a number of reasons why a person might want to talk about such an experience. He may be a loquacious person who is in the habit of talking about everything that happens to him, or he might be troubled by the experience and might want to talk about it because he hopes that he will then feel less anxious. There might be something about the experience that he does not understand, and he may hope that talking to someone about it will help him to understand it. Or it may simply be that there is something about it that demands expression, that requires that it be communicated.   The man on the cliff has told you that he would like to say more but does not have the words for it. Suppose that you realized from the tone of his voice, his facial expression, his movements, or what he said, that it might be helpful to him if he could say more. You might ask him: "Would you like to try?   Maybe I can help."

Suppose he agreed, and you then said: "You mentioned that you liked what you saw as you looked at the sea. That sounded interesting. Could you say something about what it was you saw there?" And later: "You seemed to like the way you reacted. How did you react?"

Once he realized that you were interested, he might be able to relive some of the experience with you. As he did, he might see more of the experience than he originally had, and have new reactions to it. You would be doing the kind of listening that at the Center helps people to explore and describe their experience of God.

Experiences like that of the man on the cliff seem to open a window on a new awareness of God and of oneself, and bring about new, sometimes profound, often joyful, reactions to God. Even if the person seldom, or never, adverts to them again, such experiences have their value and probably are never entirely forgotten.

Often, however, they bring with them a desire that the person either continues to remember or forgets for a while but recalls later. A desire for what? The person frequently finds it hard to say. Sometimes it is a desire for more experience at the same level of awareness; sometimes it is a desire for a repetition of the same experience or the same reactions; sometimes it is a desire for a furthering of a relationship with God that the person glimpsed in the experience.

In trying to name what it is they desire, people use terms like "integration," "more awareness," and "relationship with God." They know they want something they do not have, however uncertainly they phrase it. We will speak more specifically of this desire in Chapter 3. Just now it seems enough to say that many of the people we have met identify it to some extent with a desire for prayer.

How the Center Began

"I want to be able to pray" or "I want to be able to pray better"—these are words that retreat directors and spiritual directors hear often. They or their predecessors heard them often in the late 1960s and early 1970s too. Often the person saying them at that time believed that a lecture or a series of discussions on prayer was what he or she needed. However, if the person attended a lecture or took part in discussions, he or she might pray no more afterward than before. After a week-long discussion retreat on prayer, one person replying to a questionnaire said she had prayed only a few minutes during the entire retreat. But the desire continued to be expressed: "We'd like another talk on prayer." "What can I do to pray?"

An observer might be tempted to believe that people who talked this way, but seldom prayed, did not mean what they said. Yet the statements often seemed sincere, and frequently we knew the people making them to be truthful.

The question—"What can I do to pray?"—was more momentous than might at first appear. It referred to more than "saying prayers." The person's ability to perceive God as person rather than as a set of ideas was involved. So was his ability frankly to lay open the self to God with its experience and its affective reactions to life. When men and women say they are unable to pray, they often are referring to an inability in interior life.

What could be done to help? We will treat this question in greater detail in Chapter 6. For our present purpose, it will be sufficient to say that in the early 1970s, some of the Center's original staff had talked to a number of people about what happened when they prayed. They had, as a result, come to believe that many women and men who found it hard to pray could be helped most effectively by someone who would ask: "What would you think of trying to pray and then talking about what happens?" Or say: "Let's not talk about God. Let's talk instead about God and you. And maybe then talk about what happened the last time you tried to pray."

Such an approach represented a distinct departure from the venerable approaches of lecture and exhortation. It offered people a relationship that would continue to assist them as they took their first steps toward a new development of personal prayer.

We knew that the dynamics of this approach had to be explored and carefully investigated if we were to give consistently valuable assistance. The helping person could not expect to step casually from an instructional to a facilitative approach. He—all the first members of the staff were male—could not be a lecturer one day, and, without inner adjustment, work with people's experience the next. He would have to reflect on the different situation he would be in, listen at length, try different expedients, evaluate their results, and develop new ways of proceeding based on this experience. And—a matter of capital importance—he would also have to let his own interior reactions adjust to his new situation. It would be difficult for pastoral workers to develop this new practice without extensive collaboration with one another.

Retreat directors and other pastoral workers had very likely done on occasion what we were proposing to do. We knew, however, that it was not a usual approach and that, in effect, we were entering new territory. In particular we did not know of groups of people who had tried persistently over a number of years to explore such pastoral experience, evaluate it, and share their findings with one another in the hope that eventually this practice could contribute to new perspectives on spiritual life and pastoral practice.

We began then by inviting people to talk about God and themselves and what happened when they tried to pray. The people we talked to often found it hard to communicate on this level. They were trying to talk experientially; that is, they were trying to describe their personal experience of God. Often in the past they might have spoken of God as they would like God to be or as the catechism or their courses in theology said God was. To go beyond these languages and learn one that could express what God was actually like to them was a long and arduous process.

We have been speaking of these attempts as though they were confined to the past. They are not. Those who come for spiritual direction today also have to develop for themselves enough confidence to speak about God and themselves and must learn for themselves a personal language in which to do this. There is more awareness among Christians now than there was 20 years ago of the value of this confidence and this language. People who come for direction now often get more encouragement from their church environment than directees got then. Yet talking about God and themselves remains a new enterprise that can be both bracing and bewildering.

We have emphasized the central place of prayer in the center's ministry. Inevitably someone in an audience listening to us describe this ministry will ask: "Do you talk to people only about prayer?" We do not. Indeed, one of our most difficult tasks has been to manage to talk about prayer at all. However, a description of how one can talk realistically about what happens when a person prays, yet not talk exclusively about prayer, will best be left to Chapter 6.

How the Staff Came to Be

No description of the Center could be completely coherent without a detailed account of the original staff, the group of men who collaborated to launch the enterprise. For it is from them, from the hopes with which they began, the experience they had together, and the convictions that developed from that experience that the Center took much of the shape and vitality that have characterized it since.

However, they have not been the only people who have contributed: those who have succeeded them on the staff have also contributed to the formation of the Center as it is today. In the account to which we will devote the next few pages, then, we will begin with the original staff, but will not confine our account to their experience. We will also indicate how the staff has developed since.

The idea of a Center first began to take shape in the minds of most of the original staff during a program organized by the New England Jesuit Province in 1970 to prepare a number of Jesuits to give individually-directed retreats. The province government hoped that these retreats would attract Jesuit retreatants and would contribute to the spiritual renewal of the members of the province. These retreats were not intended for Jesuits alone, however, and, once they were made available would quickly attract other retreatants as well.

The program, which consisted of several weekend workshops, was a vivid event for a number of its participants. In New England, as well as other areas, the exploration of Christian values that accompanied Vatican Council II had produced much change. Catholics seriously interested in spiritual values found themselves facing stirring new perspectives as well as considerable confusion about spiritual life. Some asked what a Christian spiritual life was and others said it was what it had always been. Some in pained confusion rejected any attempt at formulation; others confidently proposed new ways of living a spiritual life that appeared drastically different from those to which Catholic Christians had been accustomed. In this atmosphere of diversity, and often of dispute, the individually-directed retreat showed promise of doing excellent pastoral service.

The directed retreat did not require that retreatants subscribe to a particular pattern or orientation of spiritual life. Their inspiration did not have to be Dominican, Franciscan, Jesuit, active, or contemplative; or it could be any one of them. The retreatant's life situation could be lay or priestly, or could involve membership in a religious congregation. The retreatant did not have to be Roman Catholic. He or she might not even be enthusiastic about making a retreat. All one needed was desire, enough interior freedom to pay attention to God as God appears in the retreatant's own situation, and willingness to talk to the retreat director about what happened when he or she did pay attention.

The momentum of the retreat was provided by the retreatant's desire and his or her experience of looking long and steadily at God and at what God was doing during the retreat. There was no need and little point in discussing concepts of God, of prayer, or of spiritual life. Conversations with the director focused on the experience of God taking place during the retreat, the retreatant's reaction to that experience, and the possibilities the experience opened up for further interaction with God.

The first three workshops conducted for Jesuits who would be giving directed retreats were exciting and encouraging events for many of those who participated. They addressed issues that were close to the heart of every Jesuit: one's experience of God, one's experience of Jesus, and the interior freedom the redeeming activity of Jesus brings about in the receptive person. Even more to the point, they addressed these issues not as abstract or general topics, but concretely, as they appear in people's experience. Through role-played examples, in some of which they took part themselves, participants were made keenly aware of what retreatants sound like and how they react when they recount their experience. Experiences they could expect to hear from retreatants were represented so vividly that participants were readily reminded of experiences of their own. Men would say: "We're looking here at what we're all about," and were cheered by the realization. It was not all that they were about, but it was an intimate element that they had seldom spoken of to one another. The experience evoked a bond among them that they had rarely looked at so intently.

Most of the participants in these workshops were also delighted by the possibilities the new emphasis opened up for a renewal of the retreat ministry. Some also envisioned further possibilities. The question that proved so effective a catalyst in retreats—"What happened to you when you tried to pray?"—also provided an invaluable means of giving focus to spiritual direction outside the retreat context. A practical proposal soon emerged: could some of us continue to explore together the potential of this emphasis at some sort of Center?

Those who found themselves interested in such a Center then began a series of discussions. First they explored the pastoral needs and desires of people they had encountered in their ministry. They then tried to ascertain which of those needs and desires a Center with the orientation we had in mind would be most capable of satisfying. Later in the discussions, they pondered what structures of staff development and of ministry would best enable the Center to achieve its purposes. They then took up details: Where would the Center be located? Who would staff it? How would it be financed? When could we begin?

The tone of the meeting was suffused with springtime enthusiasm. Decisions were come to by consensus, arrived at after lengthy, open-ended discussion. Several months after the discussions began, the group was ready to make definite proposals to the Jesuit provincial. The outcome of those proposals was a decision to open the Center for Religious Development.

Learning to Be a Staff

As graduates of the Jesuit course of studies in literature, philosophy, and theology, and veterans of many years of Jesuit community life, the original staff of the Center had much background in common. All of them had also had considerable pastoral experience. Here, however, the common features of their background ended and diversity began. Some had had extensive experience in retreat work and spiritual direction, while others came from quite different pastoral experience. Some had considerable background in psychology; others did not. One had a doctoral degree in clinical psychology, another a doctorate in theology. Two were professors at Weston

School of Theology, and one was the superior of the Weston Jesuit community.

They all came to the Center with the intention of contributing their expertise and vision to a common enterprise. Because it was a common endeavor, no one person's background was to exert a dominant influence and no one person's ideas were to become the Center's only ideas.

Its communal origins have left their mark on the Center. Most of our projects still carry the impression made by that early experience of extensive discussion and group decision-making. Workshops the Center sponsors are characterized by extensive interplay among staff and participants. But the most consequential impression shows itself in the present staff's continuing loyalty to group decision-making after extensive discussion.

To ensure that enough time would be available for this procedure, once the Center began, we set aside two hours a week for staff meetings. Anyone familiar with the demands made on the time of the staff at a pastoral center will recognize that this practice entailed inconvenience. Yet we have held to it. We also took a further step. We knew from our experience of other staffs with whom we were acquainted that when the pressure of everyday work becomes excessive, the first entry on the week's schedule to be questioned is the staff meeting. So we made every effort to ensure the attendance of all full-time staff members at every meeting. A firm tradition was established, so that even now, looking back over many years, we can recall relatively few occasions when a meeting was held without the presence of the whole staff and only rare occasions when a meeting was canceled.

In those first years the staff began at intervals to take one or more days away from Cambridge at a house on the seashore. There we discussed issues of policy, practice, and administration that required more time than could be allotted to them at the weekly meetings. Some decisions we wanted to make among more spacious surroundings than the city afforded, in a relaxed situation that would encourage everyone to say what he thought and felt and to change his mind if he chose to.

In the first two years the staff was entirely male and Jesuit. Even during the first year, however, we wanted a woman staff member. We felt with increasing keenness that to serve our clientéle adequately, we needed the additional experience and insight that women could bring. At that time, however, women—and men—with the qualifications we required were not easy to find. Those who were qualified were likely to be needed for other positions, as we learned when we first made inquiry of a woman we knew to be qualified. In the second year we devoted more time and energy to the quest for a qualified person who could be freed from the position she held. Eventually we succeeded. In the following years other women have joined the staff. We have become even more convinced as time has gone on that a spiritual direction center will be inadequate if its staff is made up only of men. This situation might be necessary for a short time, as it was for us, but that time should be kept as short as possible.

From the beginning we worked together as equals and avoided, as far as we could, a vertical administrative structure. Each person had an equal voice in decision-making, and we discussed issues until we came to consensus. Anyone who has had the experience of working with a group of talented, forceful people convinced both of the value of their profession or ministry and of the need for its further development knows how difficult it can be to achieve consensus in such a group. A number of circumstances have contributed to the survival of this policy at the Center. The number of full-time staff members has always been small: six at most, usually fewer. Another factor has been that, though all full-time staff people have been responsible for projects in which other staff members were not involved, there has always been a core of common responsibility.

There has been, outside this core of common responsibility, considerable diversity in the tasks to which individual staff members have devoted themselves. This variety of individual undertakings stemming from a common experience has in turn brought new experience and new challenges back to the common enterprise.

Values to Which the Staff Has Given Priority

Spiritual direction as it is understood at the Center begins with a person's willingness to disclose his or her experience of God to another person. This calls for a good deal of frankness on the part of the directee. By "experience," however, we do not mean only the objective content of the experience. The experience is not completely disclosed until the person also reveals what feelings have been excited by what has happened and the significance it has had for him or her. The high degree of frankness such disclosures require of the directee cannot be maintained—or, often, achieved in the first place—unless the directee sees that the director takes a receptive and frank attitude toward the directee's experience. With frankness on both sides so fundamental to the ministry, it is not surprising that frankness—we have usually called it openness—came to be seen as a highly desirable, even necessary attitude of staff members toward one another. If staff members disagree with one another about policy or behavior, they are expected to make the disagreement known. They are also expected to listen receptively to one another.

Such mutual frankness and receptivity, no matter how desirable, are hard to achieve. It is not always easy to recognize one's own reactions. It can be even more difficult to express them. It can be equally difficult to listen to attitudes contrary to one's own carefully enough to understand them. The task of becoming fully receptive to other staff members can be more difficult than the task of becoming receptive to the experience of directees. Most of us, before joining the staff at the Center, had spent a substantial part of our lives in situations that promoted competition. While competition bestows benefits both on the competitor and on any institution for which the competitor works, it also can instill habits of self-protection and protection of one's turf that one has to struggle against if one is to be frank with and receptive to the other members of a staff.

We have found that the effort has been worthwhile. After experiences, in the Center's early years, of disputes that aroused stronger feelings than their objective content warranted, the staff's determination to let no conflict pass without discussion kept growing stronger. This attitude of mutual frankness and receptivity has not always been fully and consistently achieved. It continues, however, to be given a high priority among the values the staff has chosen to live by.

The Developing Administrative Structure

The desire for consensus and the attitude of mutual frankness and receptivity have expressed themselves in the gradual development of an administrative structure in which each permanent staff member takes equal responsibility for the policies and management of the Center. Although the staff agreed when the Center began that each member would have an equal voice in decision-making and that all decisions of any importance would be made by the whole staff, for the first five years one of the staff acted as director of the Center. We then decided that the position of coordinator would be more consistent with the commitment all full-time staff members made to take responsibility for the Center. In 1979, after several years of working with a coordinator, we decided it was still more consistent for the full-time staff—at that time there were four members—to divide all administrative responsibilities and to work without either a director or a coordinator.

As a result of this decision, co-responsibility has become a more realistic enterprise. Earlier, if a staff member had no key administrative responsibility, it was easy for him or her to withdraw from practical concern for administration and let the director or coordinator see to it that what had to be done actually was done. Since the division of administrative responsibility, each member has participated more actively in administration. This structure has been the most satisfactory the staff has devised. "No one person in charge?" is still asked with surprise when the staff structure is described, and is sometimes voiced with a note of disbelief. The staff believes that although this is an unusual structure for pastoral centers, it is the arrangement that is most consistent with the dynamic of spiritual direction, which so strongly emphasizes the need for personal responsibility and the growth of interior freedom.

No administrative structure, of course, will ever prove entirely satisfactory. The weakness of earlier arrangements lay in the encouragement it gave our tendency to concentrate entirely on our own immediate tasks and in practice to leave crucial but less personal concerns like finances, the future, or the overall direction the Center was taking to "the person in charge." The weakness of the present arrangement is that, with no one person in charge, the well-being of the Center depends on the vitality of each staff member's vision of the Center, and on each member's personal maturity and willingness to keep growing. In particular, it depends on each member's ability and desire to cooperate rather than compete, qualities hard to come by among enterprising people. Since, however, these are qualities we have hoped for in staff members, no matter what administrative structure we work with, it seems to us appropriate that the structure itself should emphasize the necessity for them and encourage their further development.

We have taken time to describe the Center's administrative structure and the dynamics of the staff because it would be impossible to understand the Center if one overlooked the distinctive character of the staff. This one can easily do. The word "staff" itself can be misleading. It may evoke images of the assistants to a chief administrator or the employees of an institution—a mayor's staff or a library staff, for example. Neither image conveys the most important responsibilities of the Center's staff. We have often used the word "team" to describe our way of working together. But "team" too readily calls up memories of athletes with numbers on their backs. So we have continued to use "staff," with explanations like those we have just given when they have been needed.

The productive way in which the staff has often worked together is probably the Center's most noteworthy achievement. Much time and effort have been expended on its development because we have believed that an experienced, capable staff, in full voluntary agreement on the focus of our work and able to talk frankly and receptively with one another, would always be our most valuable resource. Valuable programs would be produced and inventively carried out by such a staff. Without such a staff, we would always be in some disarray and never fully accomplish what the Center is capable of accomplishing.

The achievement has been that every year three or more people with extensive experience of a ministry have freely adopted consonant approaches to it and collaborated coherently enough to develop consistent policies for the Center and enable other experienced directors who worked with them to further develop their own abilities. The working together has been constant. On most weekdays we are all in the building most of the time. It has also been close. At least twice a week we are in the same room for two hours of group reflection of different kinds. Anyone familiar with ministerial programs would agree that this is an unusual amount of time for a staff to spend together.

This amount of time spent together is a crucial element of the staff's contribution to the Center. We see our contribution to others as the contribution of learners, always in need of more knowledge and skill. Most basically, we try to learn the always-developing ways of God with God's people. Learning together and learning from one another thus form the core of our engagement with the Center.

Is the Center Jesuit?

This question deserves discussion for two reasons. It has troubled some directors who have worked with us and it pertains to the way the staff understand the nature of spiritual life.

The Center was founded by Jesuits and is incorporated as a ministry of the local Jesuit province. However, the original staff decided not to use the word "Jesuit" in the Center's title and the Center has consistently avoided using the term "Jesuit spirituality." The Center's avoidance of these terms requires some explanation.

In the 19th-century and the pre-Vatican II years of this century, terms like "Dominican spirituality," "Benedictine spirituality," "Carmelite spirituality"—derived from the names of religious orders and congregations—were in common use among Roman Catholics. The assumption underlying their popularity was that the differences among the schools of spirituality they designated were of great significance. The members of religious orders and congregations, including Jesuits, often supported this attitude.

Often, too, a school of spirituality was named after the person who had most signally propounded the elements of spirituality that the school emphasized. Writers spoke of Salesian spirituality, Teresian spirituality, and Ignatian spirituality. There was a tendency in the middle years of this century to expand verbally the number of spiritualities current in the church. "Lay spirituality" was commonly spoken of. The titles could also become more specific. One might speak, for example, of a "spirituality of lawyers," a "spirituality of physicians," a "spirituality of journalists," as though they were quite distinct from one another.

The emphasis on schools of spirituality is not as strong today as it was 30 years ago. However, it still has its proponents, particularly among some members of some religious congregations and among some of those who have learned about spiritual life from them. People still say "I practice

Benedictine spirituality," "I'm into Carmelite spirituality," or "It's Jesuit spirituality that makes sense to me."

The Center has never favored this emphasis on schools of spirituality. Some aspects of Christian spirituality are more vividly and extensively articulated in the documents of some Christian groups than they are in most Christian writings. And some aspects of Christian life have been more conspicuously practiced in some groups than among Christians in general. The emphasis on obedience to religious authority among Jesuits is one example. The emphasis on the love of poverty among Franciscans is another. These values are estimable, and have contributed incalculable richness to Christian life. However, to emphasize such differences at the Center would draw attention away from an element of Christian spirituality that the Center sees as fundamental to its ministry and common to all serious attempts to live a Christian life. We did not want to encourage people to fix their attention on what Jesuits say about obedience when it was more important for them to pay attention to their own religious experience. We had found that if we could help people to bring their personal attitudes into contact with the living God, this would give them an opportunity to live out more fully and vividly their individual vocations, no matter what those vocations were. If a man was a monk he would realize himself more fully as a monk; if a man or a woman was a lay person, he or she would tend to live out a lay vocation more fully. Because this has been our experience we have felt that we have sacrificed nothing but confusion in avoiding the term "Jesuit spirituality."

When people have been afraid that if they came to the Center for spiritual direction or for the development of their ability as spiritual directors they would end by becoming Jesuits, at least in their spiritual lives, we have believed that they were misconstruing the reality of spiritual life. They were seeing it as a body of doctrine that could be taught and studied. They were not seeing it as we were, as a progressive development of their relationship with God.

There is a historical basis for the Center's practice in this matter. Ignatius himself, for example, seems to have thought he was living and expressing Christian rather than an Ignatian or a Jesuit spirituality. For many years he did his best outside the context of a religious congregation to let God reveal Godself and to respond to God's self-revelation. The most significant lessons he learned about prayer and spiritual life he learned from his experience.

His *Autobiography* does not provide us with a model for Jesuit life. It does provide us, however, with a clear, in many instances a detailed description of how God acted with the human being named Ignatius. When we ask ourselves, while reading the *Autobiography,* what Ignatius's most prominent spiritual characteristics were, we must begin with one that was thoroughly noninstitutional: he believed in his own spiritual experience. He was not gullible. He did not rashly assume that he had experienced God. But when God let him know that this was true, Ignatius accepted God's liberality.

He also believed in himself. Beginning with a natural self-confidence, he passed through a time of near-despair and a lengthy series of other formative experiences to arrive at a developed and tested confidence in himself as the object of God's care and a person called to be a companion to Jesus.

It would be difficult to make these virtues the exclusive property of a particular religious congregation or even of a particular tradition within Christianity. Everyone who has tried to live a life of receptivity to God and response to God has had to come to terms with the most basic issues Ignatius faced. The frankness and detail with which he describes his own encounters with them can be a help to every Christian. Perhaps his greatest gift to the Church is the encouragement he offers us all to understand and accept the way God acts with each of us.

The Influence of the CRD Experience on the Staff

We began our description of the Center by discussing some of the experience that led to its inception. We also described the initial formation of the staff and the origin of some of the values by which it functions. We turn now to the questions: Have elements of the staff's experience at the Center tended to mold its members, and, if this is true, what difference has this made to them? Intense involvement in any profession or ministry tends to change its practitioners. Lawyers and physicians evince traits of personality they would not have shown so plainly if they had never practiced law or medicine. Has anything like that happened to those who have practiced spiritual direction at the Center?

Once directors begin to ask the question "What happened when you tried to pray?" and wait for an answer, spiritual direction begins to become a different experience for them. As directees gradually become more able to express their actual experience of the interaction that takes place between themselves and God, directors begin to see the relationship with God from a new perspective. They learn a great deal, for one thing, about what happens between God and people as people pray.

They find out, for instance, that often when people try to pray the effort is very brief—a few minutes long—and that they then begin to think about something else that takes their attention away from prayer. It may be an urgent problem or a concern that claims attention as soon as their minds are free of preoccupation. It may also be so trivial that the person is embarrassed to admit that it held his or her attention.

They learn, too, that there is a twilight state without specific thoughts and defined feelings that people sometimes call prayer. People who describe this state sound as though they have been gazing blankly at dense fog, but fog that shows not the slightest shift or differentiation. One director describes the state as "gazing at brown."

Directors also find that prayer often consists of almost ceaseless self-excoriation that sounds like: I have been trying to pray for a while most days, but I don't understand why I never think of God during the rest of the day. Or, I keep thinking of all the years when I paid no attention to God.

These and many other ways in which a person's desire to give attention to God is deflected and attenuated gradually make directors aware of the multitude of forces within us that can make it difficult for us to keep our attention on God for even five minutes.

Directors have known from their own experience that it is often difficult to pray, but frequently they have been only dimly aware of the difficulties themselves. They have lumped them together under the heading "distractions" or they have been so preoccupied with finding time to pray that they have given little attention to what happens when they do find time. Now they find themselves encountering the myriad concrete phenomena that make it hard for people to give their attention to God. They begin to look with fresh vision at what happens when they themselves try to pray. Then too, the multiplicity and subtle persistence of the phenomena that deflect our attention from God can gradually bring home to them that there is a touch of mystery here. Why, after all, should so many different stimuli make it so hard to pay attention to God?

Directors, then, become intimately acquainted with the struggle that often characterizes a person's attempts to give attention to God. It is important to notice that the attention of which we speak here is not the kind of attention theology students are obliged to give for the sake of their studies or a disputant in a theological argument is required to give for the sake of the argument. It is relational; that is, it is given because the person attended to is, or could become, important to the person attending. While people are intent only on exploring ideas about God, they do not commonly encounter the kind of difficulty we have been describing. These difficulties are indigenous to the world of personal relationships to which the director has been introduced.

This world, of course, contains more than difficulty. The world directors enter when they ask "What actually happened?" is far broader than difficulty. They become more conscious of how God is revealed to people.

Let us look at a fairly commonplace example of something that might happen in direction. Al is describing what his experience of prayer has been like over the last two weeks; Mary, who is doing direction with him, is listening.

Al: I've been concerned with what God might want me to do. As I look back, I suspect I haven't been praying much because I've been worried about what God might ask. Daydreaming, yes. But praying? I don't think so. So finally I faced up to it, and said: "Is there something you want?"

Mary: You asked him that straight out?

Al: Yes. But I didn't get an answer.

Mary: Oh? What happened?

Al: What happened? No answer, that's what happened.

Mary: No answer at all. Your question was just left hanging there. Tell me, Al, did anything else happen after you asked your question?

Al: I haven't thought much about anything but what God might want. So I want to say: No. But as I recall it now, I believe I felt he was close to me. I remember thinking: God's not going to leave me in a hurry.

When our section of his conversation with Mary begins, Al is giving his attention only to what God may want him to do. At the end of the exchange he has noticed that something has happened that may indicate that there is more to God's relationship with him than he has realized. Directors who listen carefully to directees notice how frequently God seems to show Godself to people and how seldom God tells them what to do. They notice, too, how often God seems more interested in the quality of the interpersonal relationship than in what the person does. Gradually those who listen to others come to grasp more of the depth of God's engagement with them and with their world. They learn to raise questions when God seems always the same to a person, when, for instance, over the past year God has invariably been seen as benignly smiling. They become aware that people experience God sometimes sad, sometimes jubilant, sometimes wistful, sometimes determined. The gospel emphasis on the primacy of what happens in a person's heart assumes a new significance when they observe God insisting on this with people who are immersed in worry about what they can and what they cannot do. Perhaps these examples are sufficient to make the reader aware that the emphasis on listening to people talk about their experience of God opens up for the spiritual director a universe of awareness of God and an acquaintance with God's ways of which the director had never been conscious.

But speaking of this experience from outside the experience itself, as the purpose of this chapter requires, cannot convey an adequate impression of the excitement, the sense of discovery, the surprise of seeing familiar things become fresh and new that the director experiences. These are currents of the atmosphere in which spiritual directors conduct their ministry that can be fully appreciated only when one has experienced them.

We have tried then to meet people not with set opinions of how God must be acting with them, but with an invitation to begin to talk about their relationship with God. The world that both director and directee enter, if this invitation is accepted, is a fresh world, much more colorful than the world depicted in the manuals of spirituality, with far more modulations of hue, atmosphere, and tone than they envision. It has its starkness. It also has adventure, joy, love, and satisfaction; and the shape these have taken and the circumstances under which they have come about always seem to be different from what we expected. It is this world that directors are committed to explore.

Frequent contact with this world has resulted in the formation of a number of attitudes that those acquainted with the work of the Center often point out. These attitudes are not always full-fledged. But they do appear, and they are noticed. What are these attitudes?

A Practical Respect for the Directee

One is a practical respect for directees that appears in a willingness to pay attention to what they say. This respect is often remarked on during workshops given for spiritual directors who have had no acquaintance with the Center. "You really paid attention to him" and "What respect you had for what she said!" are common remarks after a dialogue in which a staff member has helped a participant to describe an experience of prayer. Since those who make these remarks are usually themselves spiritual directors, the observation carries particular force. This respect, as the workshops also reveal, has consequences. The persons attended to in this way become better able to express their experience. They are enabled by this attentive listening to reveal what otherwise they might not be able to reveal, or even be aware of. An example will illustrate what we mean.

Laura is conducting a workshop on spiritual direction for a group engaged in a practical program in spirituality, and Frank, a participant, has volunteered to tell her something about his recent experience of prayer. The conversation takes place in the presence of the other participants. The purpose of the public presentation is to demonstrate the dynamics of the basic spiritual direction conversation. We begin after Frank and Laura have been talking for a minute or two.

Frank: God seems close sometimes.

Laura: Close?

Frank: Yes.

Laura: Would you like to talk about it further?

Frank: I would, but I don't know what else to say.

Laura: Well, would you like to pick a time when God seemed close? Any time recently that you recall?

Frank: I took some time to pray yesterday, and he seemed close then.

Laura: Could you say something else about what happened? You started to pray?

Frank: Yes. There was a line from a psalm that had been going through my mind. "You knit me together in my mother's womb." I let it keep going through my mind.

Laura: "You knit me together in my mother's womb." It was saying something to you?

Frank: Painstaking care and constancy. All the care God has taken.

Laura: All the care God has taken . . .

Frank: I became aware of his caring, as though he was right there, concerned about me. Funny, I remembered that he seemed close, but it's only now that I remember the concern about me. (Pause) I want to think more about that.

Laura opens the discussion that follows by asking the audience what they noticed happening during her conversation with Frank. Invariably some members of the audience will remark on the attention Laura has given to Frank and Frank's experience. They may also comment on the respect she has shown for Frank's preferences. She has asked him, for example, whether he wants to talk further about his observation that God is sometimes close to him. She has given him an opportunity to say more, but she has not pressed him to do so.

In the ensuing discussion, Frank will be asked how he experienced the conversation. He will probably say that he experienced himself invited, not dragooned, and that he found himself becoming absorbed in the memory of what had happened in the experience of prayer.

The result is a simple one, but fundamental for spiritual direction. Frank is able to see more fully and precisely what happened to him when he prayed. As a result he can decide whether to give further attention to the facet of the experience that impressed him most. Before he saw what impressed him, he had no choice.

A Practical Respect for God's Desire

The practical respect for the directee exemplified in this conversation has been complemented at the Center—gradually and over time—by an equally practical respect for God's desire to form an intimate, mutual relationship with the directee. With this there has grown in the director a conviction that such a relationship is the most important benefit that can be gained in spiritual direction. To facilitate such a relationship, to serve it without infringing on either the directee's freedom or God's freedom, becomes a director's most precious privilege.

The desire to facilitate and not determine requires of the director both patience with the vicissitudes of the directee's relationship with God and the ability to remain with the directee in empathy and hope through delays, distracting episodes, and wrong-headed choices. It also encourages the director not to substitute other services like advice-giving, problem-solving, immersion in the details of the person's routine, and exhortation, for the essential task of facilitating the relationship with God.

This desire to facilitate the relationship keeps reminding directors to attend to the directee and the directee's experience. It will help them, for example, to avoid telling lengthy stories about their own lives. These stories might be engaging, even gripping, but could distract the directee's attention from his or her own experience. The prize to be secured is the directee's relationship with God, not an opportunity for the directors to talk about themselves. There are times when only disciplined determination will enable a director to avoid distracting an appealing directee with his own or her own needs. The conviction, based on experience of giving direction, that the growth of the directee's relationship with God is of preeminent value to the directee will be a singular help to the director in developing that determination.

The willingness to strive to remain loyal to the directee's freedom also derives from this source. Without freedom no one can make the choices necessary to develop a relationship with God. The director's loyalty to the directee's freedom can result in some annoyance for a directee, especially early in the direction relationship. A directee does not always appreciate a director's habit of answering questions with "What do you think?" or "What do you want?" The director's careful, persistent encouragement to value and make use of the resources directees have within themselves, however, will gradually allow a relationship to develop between them that will enable directee and director to look together, as equals, at the directee's relationship with God and the choices available to the directee in that relationship.

Conclusion

In Chapter 1 we have sketched the origin, general purposes, and guiding principles of the Center for Religious Development. We have also set forth some of the aspects of its approach to ministry that have given it its particular character. We have not yet discussed in detail, however, the fundamental convictions that have given the Center its name. These are the strong belief that our relationship with God can mature and the complementary belief that spiritual direction can help with this maturing. Since it is from these convictions that the principal practices and policies of the Center flow, discussion of each of them deserves a chapter to itself. Chapter 2 will be devoted primarily to the former, and Chapter 6 to the second.

Chapter 2

What Is Religious Development?

Choosing a Name

Giving an enterprise its name can be a decisive step toward establishing its identity. When the name states the purpose of the enterprise, the naming may well be decisive, for then the name implies a promise. It says: This is what we intend to do.

We were in no hurry to make any more promises than we had to as we drew up plans for the Center in the spring of 1971. Eventually, however, it became inconvenient to go on talking about "it." We had to have a name that would identify our project to people who were interested, but had not taken part in the planning. So we set about making our choice. Traditional titles like the Thomas More Center and the Saint Ignatius Center we considered and dismissed. We wanted a name that would express our purpose.

We soon discovered that it was not easy to state our purpose in language that would mean to the public what we wanted it to mean.

"The Center for Spiritual Direction," for example, could seem the obvious choice. It stated what we thought we would be doing. But we knew that for many of those who saw our nameplate, "spiritual direction" would evoke images of people telling other people what to do. This was not at all what we intended, and those who came to us for that service would be disappointed.

The word "spiritual" itself, although we used it frequently, also lent itself to misunderstanding. For many people it meant "otherworldly," while we and those who came to us had this world very much in mind.

We decided to use "religious" because it looked to God but was not so open to misunderstanding. And we chose "development" because it seemed a plain, unambiguous word that pointed to the normal consequence of the work we hoped to do.

Religious development, then, the normal outcome of our work, provided the Center with its name. This term too, however, has its ambiguity. The average person living in eastern Massachusetts in the early 1970s would have thought we were talking about religious institutions, external religious observance—attendance at church services, for example—or compliance with moral precepts. We were not dismissing their importance; indeed, closer allegiance to them often resulted from the work we did. But it was the inner spiritual growth of individuals that we envisioned as the direct outcome of the work we planned to do.

Difficulties in Discussing Religious Development

One might expect that it would be a fairly simple matter to discuss the spiritual development of adults. We have found, on the contrary, that it can be an extraordinarily complex matter.

All of us who believe in God tend to have set ways of dealing with God. We have used those ways, or at least been aware of them, for some time, often since childhood. Many of us, for example, would find if we considered the matter that when we address God we make use of established prayers like the Our Father, the Hail Mary, or the Rosary, the recitation of which might well be a frequent, even a daily practice. We might also find that, when we address God less formally, in words of our own choosing, we usually do so to ask God's help. We might want this help for many reasons: we might want God to help us pass an examination, or help us succeed in a job interview. We might want God's help for a friend about to undergo an operation, or for a relative about to make a journey. We might also want help with living up to our responsibilities, or to strengthen virtues that are still weak. And we might ask God to help our world.

Prayer that asks for God's help is probably not our only informal prayer. We may thank God for help given us, or we may ask forgiveness for faults of which we are guilty. But our purposes in praying usually follow a fairly set pattern and our way of praying ordinarily does not vary much.

This tendency to be unvarying in prayer can make it hard for people to grasp what is meant when a more spontaneous approach to prayer is proposed. Their experience tells them that prayer is fixed and unvarying. The approach taken at the Center, however, envisions prayer—and with it the whole relationship with God—in quite a different way. If people encountering this approach screen out what they find unfamiliar in it and assume that, though the words are different, the reality must be what they already know, they will find it impossible to grasp what they are hearing.

Another source of misapprehension in discussions of prayer is the tendency, also deriving from past experience, to look on prayer as a duty, one of the tasks a person performs if he or she wants to be a good person. Where this motivation is strong, performance of the task is the person's intention, and what happens when the person prays is of only incidental significance.

Now that we have noted that discussions such as the one we are about to begin may have to contend with reactions in ourselves that have little to do with the content of the discussion, but a great deal to do with our own prior experience of prayer, let us take up the question of religious development. We intend to approach it as, for the most part, we have become aware of it ourselves: through the experience of directees. Our view of development will emerge from our description of this experience and the comments we make on it.

An Example of Religious Development

Let us begin with an example:

Joe, a 40-year-old Catholic, made a Cursillo six months ago.[1]

During it, for the first time in his life, he felt happy about God. God became for him a gracious and attentive father, caring and loving as God had never seemed before. Toward the end of the program Joe told Harry, one of the team, that he would like to get into the habit of praying but did not know how to go about it. Harry suggested a prayer that he called "the Jesus Prayer": "Jesus Christ, Son of the living God, have mercy on me, a sinner." He suggested that Joe choose an amount of time he could give to prayer every day, and that during that time he recite the prayer quietly and thoughtfully, establishing a rhythm with the words. There would be times, Harry remarked, when Joe would want to pause at a particular word or phrase, and let it sound in his heart for a while. At other times it would be enough just to go on repeating the prayer. As they finished talking, Harry said: "Nothing could be more simple, but it will make a difference between God and you if you keep at it."

Joe began to say the Jesus Prayer. He knew he needed Jesus' mercy, and he enjoyed asking for it. After a few days he decided to allot 15 minutes every day to the Jesus Prayer.

---

1.   Joe, like the other "persons" whose experience we describe in our examples, does not exist as an individual human being. His life has been drawn from the lives of thousands of people we have known in the course of our ministry, and his experience from their experience. To the extent that he reminds readers of people they know and his experience rings true to experience with which they are acquainted, he is a valid figure for our purposes.

He found it easy to give the time, and the 15 minutes passed quickly.

After a few weeks, however, it became more difficult to keep his attention on what he was saying. Sometimes he was so distracted that when he finished he could not recall having prayed. He recognized that the Jesus Prayer had begun to bore him. "Maybe," he said to himself, "all that's needed is a little more willpower." At the same time, family needs and the demands of his work often seemed to require all his attention, so that it became increasingly difficult to spare the time for prayer. One morning, several months after the Cursillo, Joe realized that he had not prayed for a week. The realization startled him at first; then he wondered: "What about this time I've been taking for prayer? Am I asking too much of myself?"

This was the beginning of a debate within himself. Back and forth it went, sometimes settling on his family's need for his presence, sometimes focusing on the possibility that what he had begun would eventually prove valuable, at other times circling around the thought that no one else he knew gave this much time to private prayer. In the course of this interior argument, he remembered one day that Harry had said: "It can make a difference between God and you if you keep at it." "If," Joe groaned. "Now I know why he said 'if'." In a quiet hour Joe managed to find for himself, he suddenly recalled how new, how fresh God had seemed at the end of the Cursillo. He also took into account how difficult prayer had become and how hard it was to find time for it. After considering for some time, he finally said: "It's worth the trouble." After that he became more successful at finding time for prayer, and continued with the Jesus Prayer.

One morning, as he said the phrase "the living God," he heard each syllable ring in his mind like the note of a bell: *the living God*. The phrase rang for a moment, then went on echoing for the next half-hour. It thrilled him, and as the echo continued he became more and more delighted. For weeks he enjoyed repeating the phrase and listening to it. Sometimes it rang in clear, distinct notes; sometimes the notes were more subdued. It always seemed to be saying something beyond the words that stirred him, though he could never quite make out what it was. It became easier to find time to pray, and he found himself experiencing a growing happiness. One evening his wife remarked that he had become less irritable and easier to get along with. He had not noticed this himself, but since his wife was a keen observer of his moods, he thought there must be something to what she said.

Praying one morning, he repeated aloud the words "the living God" very slowly. Pausing between syllables as he often did now, letting his ears and his mind be filled with the words, he remembered something that had happened a few weeks earlier. Walking alone, he had slipped under the low-lying bough of an immense tree that stood in a park near his home. It was early August, and the tree was opulent with late-summer foliage. Looking up, he found himself gazing into a limitless height of gently, soundlessly stirring leaves. It occurred to him that the tree was like a world, providing welcome and shelter to more birds, small animals, and insects than he could see, but that nevertheless made their homes there. He reflected too that the tree was welcoming him into that world, that it was offering him shade, movements of cool air, and access to an abundance of life. To all of these he had been a stranger before he entered that world; he would still be a stranger to them if he had not stepped under its boughs. Joe said to himself: "The tree is like God. He's full of life, and he has invited me to take shelter in that life."

Now, as he prayed, the memory of the tree returned. Again he gazed up at the lush masses of sheltering foliage rising endlessly above him. He wondered again at the ceaseless motion of the leaves. It seemed to him that the life of God was palpably there above and around him, calling his attention to itself, yet letting him know too that he could never fathom it. "There is always more to it," he thought. Exhilarated, he repeated the words "the living God" over and over. Then, abruptly, he realized that a change had taken place in the way he said the words. He was no longer musing over them and, unable to contain the wonder and appreciation he felt, was addressing the words to God.

Comments on the Example

Now that we have described Joe's experience of prayer over the months since he made the Cursillo, let us pause to consider the changes that have taken place during that time in his prayer and his attitudes outside prayer. The following are those that seem most significant to us.

1. The character of Joe's decision-making changes. His first decision is a simple resolution to recite the Jesus Prayer frequently, one that he makes without apparent hesitation. Later, after he has experienced distractions, boredom, and the difficulty of finding time, and has become familiar with his own vacillation, he comes to a better-informed decision to continue with the Jesus Prayer.

2. A new focus emerges spontaneously in the prayer when Joe becomes aware of the phrase "the living God" ringing distinctively and compellingly in his consciousness.

3. The prayer takes on a new dimension when Joe experiences happy excitement as "the living God" rings in his mind.

4. Joe assents to the new direction the prayer has taken and furthers it by recalling the phrase and repeating it to himself.

5. He also allows himself to continue to experience a growing happiness.

6. Prayer continues to change for Joe. Most recently, the memory of what happened under the tree adds to his awareness of the life of God.

7. Until he recalls the experience under the tree, Joe in his private prayer has addressed God only in the formal words of the Jesus Prayer. As he recalls his experience under the tree, however, he uses the words "the living God" to express his wonder and appreciation to God.

8. Changes have taken place in Joe's demeanor without his noticing them. He has become more tranquil. He has also become more relaxed and agreeable in his behavior toward his family.

Some of these changes may seem commonplace, even trivial. Yet all of them represent either points of development in Joe's prayer or points of development in his daily behavior outside prayer. Every change that takes place in us and in our endeavors is not, of course, development. Some changes represent decline; others are regressive. What makes these particular changes developmental? We will answer by exploring further each of the changes we have noted and then commenting on the overall progression that, taken together, they present to us. In our exploration and comments we will have in mind that none of Joe's experiences are idiosyncratic, but resemble the experiences of many people who engage in a continuing attempt to pay attention to the living God in their lives. The details are individual and the progression is more clearly delineated than it often appears in people's lives, but the impulses they illustrate are often experienced.

Let us begin our exploration with Joe's principal decisions to pray. The first, made as a result of his experience of the Cursillo, was a simple decision to recite the Jesus Prayer frequently. The account does not indicate whether he was motivated at this time by desire, by a sense of obligation, by social pressure (Who doesn't resolve to pray after a spiritual renewal program?), or by a combination of all three. Joe probably was not aware of all the elements that entered into his decision to pray frequently. It is likely that he did not think much about what prompted him.

Months later, he made a decision to go on praying. This decision, however, was substantially different from the first. It involved a determination to come to grips with distractions, make his way through boredom, and find time when time would be hard to find. Anyone who has experienced both kinds of decision-making knows how different they are. When he made the first decision, Joe did not know what he was getting into. When he made the second, he had experienced struggle, and knew he would experience it again.

When Joe made his second decision, he knew that what he was deciding would entail effort, mistakes, and disappointment. Why then did he make the decision? Why did he give himself this aggravation?

Joe would answer by saying something like: "It seemed worth it" or "If you want to get, you have to give." The business world has taught him that to receive dividends he has to invest, and his experience has now made him aware that if he expects prayer to be a rewarding practice, he will have to invest in it. God had seemed fresh and new during the Cursillo, and Joe had felt vital as a result. If God is to continue to be fresh and new and he himself is to feel vital, he will have to invest in prayer. What has to be invested is time, energy, interest, and probably other personal resources. Joe has, in short, decided to invest something of himself. When such a commitment is made, prayer becomes a more personal enterprise, freely embarked upon, very different from "something I ought to do" or "something everybody does."

The Content of Prayer Changes

The content of Joe's prayer changed spontaneously when one phrase in the Jesus Prayer was suddenly brought into relief for him. The phrase was not the one he had thought was most significant. "Have mercy" had seemed to him the core of the Jesus Prayer, and it was this petition for mercy that he had been emphasizing. The sudden emergence into vivid consciousness of the words that spoke directly of God offered a new focus for Joe's attention. Indeed, the words, ringing so attractively and persistently, seemed to call out for his attention.

This episode can teach Joe an important fact about prayer. It can let him know that what happens when he prays is not always what he makes happen or wants to happen. The point of prayer is not to be always in control. Far from it. If he learns to be receptive to the unexpected image, insight, or feeling that surfaces while he is praying, Joe can let himself be more receptive to God's influence in his prayer.

There is nothing astonishing about this emergence into vivid consciousness of "the living God." God may be directly influencing Joe's prayer in the incident of the ringing phrase, but there is nothing in the account that compels him or us to assert that God did. One thing, however, seems clear: Joe himself did not consciously induce the ringing of the phrase. It happened to him.

If Joe takes this incident seriously, he may recognize that committing himself, not simply time, to prayer involves relinquishing some control over what happens in prayer. He can come to recognize that listening to and looking at what happens unexpectedly can be as important as, or even more important than, anything he thinks or says in prayer.

It is important to note here that Joe is not being invited to introspection. Introspection is examination of oneself. What Joe heard directed his attention to God, not to himself. What seemed to say more than he could grasp was a phrase about God: "the living God." Indeed, if he keeps attending to it he may come to know God better, may realize, for example, that God is full of life and is inviting him to keep gazing at all that life.

Not everyone allows himself or herself to pay attention to new experiences in prayer. There are obvious reasons for this reluctance. New experiences can alter our perceptions of our environment. They can also change our perceptions of God. In the depths of ourselves we may not be ready to let such changes take place. If this is so, we might not listen as Joe did or recall later what the experience was like. There is something of will, a touch of decision, in letting oneself listen as Joe listened. He did not have to do so. And once he did, he did not have to continue to listen. He chose to listen, and to continue to listen. Nor did Joe stop there. He kept recalling the phrase and repeating the words. In doing so he kept putting himself in the way, not of repeating the original experience—for no experience can be repeated—but of hearing the phrase say more than he originally heard.

Joe's Feeling-Reactions

We have commented on Joe's willingness to pay attention to a new and unanticipated occurrence in prayer and the steps he took to keep giving his attention to it. Another aspect of this experience also deserves consideration. Joe reacted to the phrase with feeling as well as perception. He perceived the phrase and the ringing. He also experienced the psycho-physical reaction we call "feeling." Joe heard "the living God" with delighted excitement. Many of us concentrate so exclusively on our perceptions and thoughts that we are hardly aware that our feelings are reacting to what we perceive. Yet our perceptions bring about feeling-reactions in us, and the more important the perception is to us, the more pronounced the feeling is likely to be. Our bodies as well as our minds react to our experiences of God. And these reactions affect the way we relate to these experiences. When Joe feels excitement and delight in reaction to "the living God," these reactions give a depth and richness to the experience that awareness alone would not give. This depth provides the seedbed in which the experience can give rise to memories and new images. Of still greater importance, however, are the relational consequences of these reactions. Our feelings and emotions can bring us into association with a person we may be contemplating as our awareness alone cannot.

It may seem surprising that we should include among the significant changes that take place in Joe's prayer his willingness to enjoy "the living God" and to let himself feel the growing happiness that follows. Is it conceivable that a person might not let himself or herself experience such agreeable feelings? In prayer people can shy from joy as they shy from other strong feelings. They often experience such feelings as hazardous, and either consciously or subconsciously defend themselves against them. They control the feelings by refusing to let themselves consciously experience them. The price they pay for this control is a lack of engagement with the experience. By letting himself feel the joy and growing happiness, Joe has surmounted a barrier that could have kept him from a deeper engagement with prayer. He could have allowed the emergence or persistence of joy to create a predicament that would have interfered with the spontaneous movement of his prayer. Because he did not, he is now in a position to learn from experience that strong feelings need not detract from prayer, that they can instead contribute to it.

Joe's attention is held by the phrase "the living God" over a longer span of time than he would have thought possible. Then, unexpectedly, the phrase burgeons into the memory of his experience under the immense tree, and the memory begins to speak to him in a new, more tangible way about the life of God and the invitation that life is offering to him. It is as though the phrase has taken on body, and has done so by unlocking a capacity for remembering and imaging that previously was not at the service of his prayer. Through his memory and the image his memory presents to him he is able to let more of himself enter the prayer.

It may strike the reader as singular that only in the last of the incidents we described does Joe address the living God directly. We might well ask: How has he managed to avoid doing so? Here we touch on the mystery that often shows itself in prayer. For this slowness in coming to speak directly to God is a characteristic many of us share with Joe. We do not hesitate to address God in set, formal prayers—the Lord's Prayer, the Eucharistic Prayers, or the Jesus Prayer, for instance. Nor does this hesitation usually appear when we ask God for help. But it often does appear when what we have to say to God expresses something we perceive as intimately our own.

When Joe finally speaks out his wonder and appreciation to God, he does so by repeating the words that have excited his wonder and appreciation. He is obviously making no attempt to be eloquent. He is simply expressing his reaction to what he has seen of God as candidly as he can, without elaboration or ornament. We must not allow the simplicity of his expression to obscure the significance of what he has done, however. Joe's posture in prayer has for some time been receptive. He has listened to "the living God" and accepted both what he has heard and his reactions to what he has heard. Now, although he remains receptive, he also speaks out to God. He expresses to God what is in his heart. In doing so he begins to reveal himself to God.

The changes we have commented on so far have taken place in Joe's prayer. When Joe's wife tells him that he has become easier to get along with, however, she calls his attention to a change she has observed in his everyday relational behavior. Joe is surprised at her remark. He has not been trying to effect such a change, and has not been aware that it was taking place. Like most of us, he has assumed that his personal relationships improve only when he or the other people involved deliberately set out to improve them. But now a change seems to have taken place without any effort having been made to achieve it. If Joe considers the spontaneity of this change, he may find himself wondering whether prayer as he is experiencing it will change other aspects of his behavior too.

What Development Has Taken Place?

Let us step back now from the individual experiences we have discussed and take a more comprehensive look at what has happened to Joe since he completed the Cursillo. Often when we give workshops on spiritual direction we present, usually through role-plays, a sequence of experiences something like those we have just discussed, and then ask the participants what seems most significant about what they have witnessed.

The comments frequently sound like these:

"He (or she) is trying to cope with a poor self-image."

"Effective carrying-out of a significant project."

"Powerful movement toward self-acceptance."

"Increasing vulnerability."

After the participants have made their comments, we usually say:

"Fair enough. You've been impressed by indications of personal maturity and personal development. Did you notice anything else?"

The comments are appropriate replies to our question. They represent what many participants in these workshops see as the most important aspect of the experience: the personal growth of the individual. This growth does take place, and it is significant. Something else takes place, too, both in the workshop presentations and in Joe's experience. This something else has to do with God. More precisely, it has to do with what happens between the person and God.

Let us look more closely at this aspect of Joe's experience. Joe's desire when he begins to say the Jesus Prayer we have left vague—as vague as it is to Joe himself. It is clear enough, though, that he wants something other than psychological well-being. Joe wants the enlivenment he experienced during the Cursillo to continue. He knew from the religious instruction he has received that prayer is a duty of Christian life and one of the important ways a Christian can show appreciation and reverence for God. During the Cursillo he came to see God as a loving and caring father and wants that awareness to continue. Frequent prayer seems a way of ensuring that it will. It will also, he hopes, help him get the inspiration he will need to live motivated by God's love.

Joe soon learns, as do most of us who set out to pray, that the initial motivation generated by an experience like a Cursillo or a retreat is not enough to keep him praying. He discovers that he has to keep giving something of himself to prayer if he is to continue. First he gives the willingness to persist in the teeth of boredom. Then he gives the effort to find time when time is not easily come by. Later, when prayer abruptly takes new, unexpected directions, Joe gives over his sense of being in charge of the direction the prayer will take. He allows his feelings to be stirred by what he hears and sees, and so lets this involuntary dimension of himself become engaged. Finally, he begins to entrust to God his unguarded feeling-reactions by expressing them spontaneously.

It is easy to see that Joe's role in his experience of prayer has changed gradually from arbiter and determiner to receiver and responder. He still has the power to stop praying. He also has the capacity to dismiss new changes that present themselves to him. But what happens in the prayer is less often what he has planned and more frequently what is unexpected.

To the extent that Joe is Everyperson—and each of us has to decide whether he represents Everyperson for him or her—we all face the possibility of such a progression while we persist in giving ourselves frequently to prayer. Whether consciously or not, we begin with the impression that we are in charge of what happens when we pray and gradually come to recognize that this is no longer so. Prayer becomes dialogic. It cannot become a conversation between equals, of course. Nor does it become dialogue in the sense in which a conversation between humans can be dialogue: I ask you a question, and you reply, or you make a statement and I agree, disagree, or avoid the issue. It becomes dialogue rather in the sense that the praying person ceases to control the course of the prayer and what happens can be initiated by someone else. Prayer becomes a situation in which sometimes at least we communicate with God and invite God to communicate with us.

Although we are talking here about dialogue in prayer, we do not mean to dismiss the dialogic aspect in all of life. God communicates through what is and what happens, though not in the simplistic way we sometimes ascribe to God, and we react. There is no impermeable wall between what happens in prayer and what happens in the rest of life, as Joe learned from his wife's comment about the change that had occurred in some of his attitudes and behavior. Just now, however, we want to concentrate on the dialogue that happens in prayer, while acknowledging that it is not only in prayer that this dialogue occurs.

The Contemplative Attitude

When the phrase "the living God" seizes Joe's attention and holds it, a crucial change takes place in his prayer, a change that then becomes the basis for further changes. Up to that time his prayer has consisted largely of the recitation of a formula. From that time on it centers on listening to words which describe God. What is there about the phrase and the attention he accords it that makes so much difference to him?

The phrase says something about God that attracts Joe. He listens; that is, he does not try to determine what the phrase means but simply listens and lets his feelings react. He comes to realize he does not understand the phrase completely, but he does not try to satisfy his curiosity. He simply lets himself become absorbed in what he hears. As he listens, absorbed, what he hears takes a hold on his heart.

This kind of listening—or looking—has as its object not information but knowledge of the other. Becoming absorbed in the other, it seeks to allow the other to reveal itself, its life, to the one who is listening or looking. It is contemplative in that it does not pry knowledge from the other, but waits attentively for the other to reveal itself.

The ability to contemplate persons and things is natural to us. Although some of us are more inclined than others to make use of it, the most activity-prone among us have experienced times when the face of someone we loved has held our absorbed attention for appreciable periods of time. Mothers have no difficulty understanding what we mean by contemplation when they recall their first opportunity to look at a child to whom they have just given birth.

This ability to look or listen contemplatively is at the heart of any prayer that is developing toward being more receptive to God. What it is that shows God to us for our contemplation varies widely from one person to another, and from one set of circumstances to another in the life of any one person. Joe found to his surprise that a phrase in a prayer provided a window through which he could contemplate God. Later the memory of his experience under the tree provided him with another window. Phrases, statements, passages from Scripture, memories, a person's experience of nature, encounters with people, his or her experience of the sacraments and the liturgy all can serve as windows through which a person can contemplate God.

Frequently in our technique-conscious culture, the looking and listening we have described are confused with the amount of time a person might take to look and listen. Someone might react to this discussion by saying: "I can't give an hour to prayer every day." It is true that we cannot contemplate without taking time to contemplate. It is not the amount of time we spend that matters, however, but looking at or listening to receptively. Three minutes might often be long enough to look. A half-hour might not be long enough if during that time we are unable to look or listen receptively.

What we see when we look contemplatively elicits feeling-reactions, and feelings tend to move us to expression. When we express our feelings to a person to whom our feelings are reacting, we show the person something of our inner life. This is a way bonds are formed between persons and, when a bond already exists, it is a way the bond is strengthened and given deeper roots. On our part, this capacity to form bonds by expressing our feelings to the other person enables us to form, strengthen, and root more deeply our bond with God.

Further Development

Two more moments of development now have to be described and discussed. Both occur so frequently that no treatment of development which omitted them could be considered adequate. To describe them, we will return to Joe. A month after he recalled his experience under the tree, Joe's prayer becomes distracted and lifeless. When he first notices this change, he thinks he is simply having a bad day. But the bad day proves to be a harbinger. Recitation of the Jesus Prayer wearies him. Even "the living God" has become just words.

I must be doing something wrong, he thinks. Maybe I'm not trying hard enough. So he throws himself into the effort to quell distractions. He finds, though, that struggling with distractions is like swatting mosquitoes on a sultry evening. No sooner has he disposed of one than another takes its place. He also tries extending the time he gives to prayer. But the longer prayer proves to be just as insipid.

It then occurs to Joe that ignorance might be the source of the problem. I don't know enough about prayer, he says to himself. So he chooses several books from the parish bookstand and begins to read them in the time he has devoted to prayer. After a few days, however, he feels uneasy. I'm welshing, he thinks. But he does not know what else to do.

That Sunday at the Eucharist, the priest speaks of Jesus' invitation to ask for what we want. After each of his comments, he repeats the word "Ask!" That afternoon, as Joe reads the Sunday paper, the word keeps echoing in his mind. "Ask!" He begins to remonstrate: Why would I have to ask? I've been asking. Doesn't God know what I need? But the word continues to sound: "Ask!"

He asks. Alone in the house he says to God: "Why is this happening to me? Why can't I pray?" He stops and thinks, then says to himself: I'm asking questions, but I'm not asking. He then says to God: "I need your help. Help me, please." That seems closer to what he wants to say. He goes on: "I want to pray, to have you mean more to me."

Joe pauses, and thinks: there's something else I want to say. He says: "I'm stopped. And I'm disappointed. You did seem to be making me more aware of you. Now, no matter how hard I try, you still seem far away. I've been getting nowhere, and I'm becoming resentful." Resentful? He thinks with a start: I guess I am resentful. How can you say to God that you're resentful? But I am, so I'd better say it. He says to God: "I'm not proud of it, but I resent the way you seem to have led me on, and then disappeared. I would be better off if you had never shown me what you can be to me."

The strength of the feelings that animate him as he says this takes Joe by surprise. The surprise, however, does not stop him. He goes on to do everything he can to make sure that God hears from him what it is like for him to be discouraged, disappointed, and resentful. Several times he stops and asks himself whether he is being petulant, but he overrides his hesitation, and keeps on until he is satisfied that he has expressed everything that is in him that has to do with his impasse.

It is only later, when he thinks back on what has happened, that he realizes that at some point in his speaking to God he became aware that he was being listened to, and listened to with understanding.

What Has Happened?

Reflection will make it clear that in the course of this experience, Joe has changed again. We could overlook the pivotal element in the change by giving all our attention to determining whether he has received what he sought. Of course, from one point of view, he has not. He is not experiencing the imagery or the feelings of joy, exhilaration, and growing happiness he experienced earlier. When he asked God to help him to pray he expected that, if God answered his request, the prayer would be accompanied by both imagery and feelings like those he had become accustomed to. This has not happened. Something else has happened, however, that he did not expect.

He had expressed himself spontaneously to God on the earlier occasion when he recalled the experience under the tree. At that time, he used the phrase "the living God" to show his wonder and appreciation to God. Anything approaching candid, spontaneous expression of whatever he knew to be in his heart has, however, remained foreign to him. In particular, he has never expressed rankling feelings to God. Now, however, by expressing his disappointment, resentment and fear so frankly, he notably broadens the range of his self-disclosure. As he does so, he recognizes that he is being listened to.

Neither the request nor the self-disclosure has come easily. Each represents for Joe a further departure from reliance on himself in prayer. Each represents, too, another movement toward a firmer reliance on God and on God's vision. It would be hard to exaggerate the difficulty most of us experience in seriously petitioning God to help us out of an impasse like Joe's. It would also be hard to overstate how important it is to do so if we are to keep developing in prayer. People in Joe's predicament sometimes spend months futilely trying to reason their way out of it. They—we—behave like the four-year-old who goes through most of the motions of swimming while carefully keeping one foot on the bottom of the pool. Joe does not know why it took him so long to ask. But he does know that when he did ask, something changed in the way he experienced himself before God. It is not that he has been unaware that, like every other created being, he depends on God. Nor has he hesitated to acknowledge his dependence. He has not hesitated to ask for God's help in other situations—when, for instance, his mother was seriously sick, or when he was baffled by the truculent behavior of one of his sons. But asking God candidly to help him with prayer that has gone awry is a far more formidable prospect.

The Developing Relationship with God

It has become increasingly clear that important elements of Joe's prayer take their major significance from the fact that they further his relationship with God. The last two moments we described—asking God and, in the context of asking, expressing his rankling feelings to God—make the relational movement of his prayer especially evident.

God has a relationship with each of us, and has it whether we know it or not. God is Creator to all of us, whether or not we recognize the fact. God is the Sustainer of life, even when individuals remain unaware this bond exists between God and them. We are not suggesting, therefore, that there was no relationship between God and Joe before Joe made the Cursillo. We are suggesting, though, that the relationship was capable of further development, and that development has been taking place.

Viewed from another perspective, Joe's relationship with God has become more explicit. What he knew before in a routine, largely implicit way he now knows in a new, fresh way. He now knows as discoverers know, and he reacts as discoverers do.

No one would call the events we have described spectacular. There is a homely look to developmental experience. Development shows itself in people as they are, with their attitudes and doubts, their ability to relate, and their difficulties in relating. There is little flash to development. Joe could easily say:

I'm surprised that the realization that God is living suddenly came to mean so much to me. It seems obvious when I think about it.

"It seems obvious." "Why didn't I think of it before?" "Wouldn't anyone feel this way?" These remarks represent the kind of reaction one often hears from people who have just recounted experiences like Joe's.

Development can be so homely that a person hearing it described can easily overlook its importance. Indeed, the person experiencing the development can also overlook its importance.

Some of Joe's experiences, however, are foundational. They provide ground on which further development of his explicit relationship with God can take place.

For one thing, he has learned to give steady attention to God. More precisely, he has listened to the phrase "the living God" lengthily and repeatedly, so that he has been able to contemplate God through this "window." Other people will contemplate God through other windows: objects of the natural world, for example, memories of incidents in their lives that seem to reveal God's action, or biblical or liturgical texts. Joe himself has also made use of memory. Now that he has learned to look long and steadily at God, he can bring this ability to bear through other windows. He may also find that the number of windows available to him will keep increasing.

He has been attracted to the living God. God has become someone to him, not simply a faceless being who can do him favors and get him out of difficulties. If you said to him, "It's useful to have God in your life," he might answer, "Yes, but there's much more to it than that." The "more to it" provides him with a basis for relationship that usefulness could never provide.

Joe's experience has also introduced him to a God who strives to give more body to the relationship with Joe. This God does by inviting Joe progressively to commit more of his personal resources to the relationship. Not content with Joe's vivid awareness of "the living God," a broader range of responses and a growing reliance on God to continue the development of their relationship, has gradually been called forth.

In our account of Joe's experience, we have tried to describe what it can be like for a person to begin to develop a more explicit relationship with God. The development we have described is limited in its extent. It takes place over a relatively short period of time, and does not include elements that one might expect to make their appearance in a person's later experience.

The circumstances and content of every person's development are unique. Another person's development might begin in quite different circumstances and its content might exhibit quite different features. Religious development does not have to be complete, or even extended, to be genuine development.

Joe has come to see God differently; he is aware of God on a deeper level of his consciousness; he reacts affectively to God in new ways; he relies on God more. Some of his attitudes to people important to him have begun to change as his prayer changes. Joe's relationship with God can go on developing. But he has begun, and his relationship is developing.

Spiritual Direction at the Service of Religious Development

Up to this point in this chapter on religious development, we have not spoken of the contribution that one-on-one, continuing spiritual direction can make to religious development. The omission has been intentional. It seemed an apt way to make clear to the reader that religious development as we have described it can and does take place without the assistance of spiritual direction. It seemed an apt way, in other words, of giving to both religious development and spiritual direction their proper place in relation to one another. Both development and direction will have prominent places in later chapters of this book. Let us close this chapter then by saying a few words about the relationship between them.

Spiritual direction neither originates nor gives shape to a person's religious development. Basic to spiritual direction as we understand it is the awareness that long before any spiritual director made an appearance in a person's life, God was there and was at work. Spiritual direction presupposes that God is acting in the life of the person who comes for direction. It also presupposes that, if direction is to benefit a person, he or she wants a more explicit relationship with the God who has been there in his or her life and has been at work.

What, then, does spiritual direction contribute? First of all, it serves. It places itself at the service of the relationship between the directee and God and of the development of the relationship that God has put underway.

Spiritual direction facilitates the explication of the relationship and so of its development. Listening to a person's desire and helping him or her to explore it can help the person identify and solidify his or her desire. Looking with a person at his or her experience of God, at his or her attempts to develop the relationship with God, and at what happens as a result can help the person to proceed with keener perception and steadier assurance.

Is not spiritual direction, then, a humble ministry? It is.

Chapter 3

Those Who Come for Direction: Desire and Commitment

Introduction

Chapters 1 and 2 have described the Center and the view of religious development found there. Against that background we introduce in this chapter those who come for direction and, in Chapter 4, the participants in the associates' program who do much of the directing.

There are three principal ways in which directees choose to make themselves known at the Center. To some extent when they request direction, and more extensively after they have begun direction, they say who they are as they see themselves, why they have come to the Center, and what they hope will happen for them there. As they speak, it is clear that they see themselves as ordinary people whose lives mirror the lives of their neighbors.

Directees also make themselves known through the informal assessments that take place on several occasions before and during direction. The format of these assessments has developed over the years as both the staff and the associates have learned how to be more helpful to directees. The first takes place during the introductory interview. The person, assisted by the interviewer, assesses his or her ability to invest in the process of direction. Later, after direction is underway, the person, with the help of the director, determines whether

her or his relationship with God is indeed becoming more fruitful. Toward the end of the year, if the direction continues that long, the directee in a third assessment says as clearly as he or she can what has happened during the year and how productive the experience has been.

The third way the directee becomes known takes place through the relationship between the directee and God. The key moments that can occur in that relationship will be given specific attention in Chapter 9.

Preambles to Direction

Beginning in mid-August, a steady flow of telephone calls signals the start of each new year at the Center. Everyone who calls inquiring about direction receives a letter to be read at leisure. Prospective directees are asked to contact the Center again if reading the letter has affirmed their desire for direction. The decision to pursue the inquiry rests with the person.

The Letter

Dear Friend:

We are happy to have your inquiry about receiving spiritual direction at the Center for Religious Development.

Many more people are looking for direction than we can accomodate. This obliges us to devote our limited time and energy to the process involved. For this reason we want to share with you the following information about direction as it is done here at CRD.

1. Spiritual direction is of assistance to many but not to everyone. It can be more helpful at some times than at others. For example, someone may sincerely desire to pray and yet at a particular period in life simply not have the time or energy to do so. Because of this, prospective directees are asked to discuss their reasons for wanting direc-

tion and their present availability in an introductory interview, and to participate in an assessment with the director after about seven visits. If direction does not seem beneficial, the interviewer or director works with the applicant to discover what might be more helpful.

2. The director would assist you to talk about what happens when you try to pray. Because our life and our prayer are bound together, life problems would be discussed, but always in the context of prayer that has taken place or will take place.

3. One of the major assumptions for our practice of spiritual direction is that God communicates directly with individual people. Our directors help persons to notice how God's personal presence appears in their lives, and help them to consider how they want to respond to that personal presence.

4. Direction is not a substitute for either counseling or therapy. Spiritual direction can be very beneficial while a person is also engaged in counseling or therapy, but careful consideration must be given to the potential helpfulness in individual situations. This discussion would have to take place at the introductory interview.

5. Directees come for direction on a weekly basis at least until the assessment. Directees coming for the first time often continue weekly direction for the first year.

Our directors are qualified and competent in their ministry. They are people of mature age—late 30s to late 60s—who have had experience in spiritual direction or in some other one-to-one setting where the development of spiritual life has been an important part of the process. They are not beginners. Many are taking time out from their usual ministries to spend a year as associates with the permanent CRD staff in order to deepen and broaden their abilities. During the year their ministry with us is critiqued and supervised.

We do not ask for or accept payment for spiritual direction. Direction is a service we give gladly toward the growth of the spiritual life of those who come to us. However, we are responsible for the maintenance and administration of a sizeable establishment. The permanent staff helps the center meet expenses by giving directed retreats, workshops, and development programs. Directors who are with us for the year contribute through the payment of tuition for their supervised ministry.

We ask that those coming for spiritual direction also give a contribution toward the maintenance and administration of the Center. We have no set amount in mind, but do ask that a just and fair contribution be given. We appreciate receiving these offerings during the Christmas and Easter seasons. Some cannot afford to make any financial contribution, and we understand this. Everyone is welcome. We simply ask that those who are able to give do so.

If, after reading this, you would like to talk about receiving spiritual direction at the Center, please call during regular work hours (9:00 a.m.-4:30 p.m., Monday through Friday). We would be happy to arrange an introductory interview with one of the staff.

Sincerely,

The CRD Staff

The next step is the introductory interview conducted by a staff member or a graduate of CRD. Before seeing what happens during that hour, we should stop and consider the people who come and what they want.

What Do People Say They Want?

People come with differing personalities and needs. One is personable and articulate. The next is shy and timid. Patience is needed to help each one begin to say clearly what he or she wants. There is an amazing variety of initial reactions to the question: "What is it that you hope for from spiritual direction?"

Rita will say: I'm not certain that I want to know God better but I do need something in my life to make it worthwhile.

Denny comments: My life seems empty. I feel a void inside myself needing to be filled. I'm giving out all the time but there's nothing coming in.

Louise remarks: I'd like to talk to someone on a regular basis. I try to pray but God seems rather vague to me. Maybe talking about it could help me.

Mike tells his interviewer: My life has been pretty hectic. For a couple of years I was drinking too much and experimenting with drugs. Even while I was doing that I was trying to help other people who were in pain. I could really see good and evil operating in my life. I think I'm in the process of choosing what's good and I need to be more in touch with God.

These men and women, and others like them, will often go on to say that they have had some experience, no matter how slight, that makes them think that God wants to be present to them. They sense intuitively that this experience is not self-induced but has its source in God.

Their words and their experience serve as the starting point for a discussion in which the applicant, with the help of the interviewer, searches out and determines his or her ability to invest in the process of direction at this time. This is precisely the reason for the interview.

Some Signs of Readiness for Direction

Itemizing all possible signs of readiness could be an endless task. However, we want to look at some signs that experience has proven to be most significant. These are desire or motivation, perseverance or commitment, and the ability to develop relationships. Here is how the interviewer tries to discover whether these characteristics are present and to what degree.

1. Desire/Motivation

As the interviewer listens, he or she becomes rather quickly conscious that all these women and men are saying in one way or another that they have desire. They do want something. If applicants are not accustomed to speaking of religious matters or not used to telling another what their deepest longings are, they can seem inarticulate or vague, even somewhat disorganized in their thought and feeling. Interviewers may find that the primary task is to help them clarify the desire or motivation in order to determine whether or not that desire can be met and satisfied through spiritual direction.

If the desire for a growing relationship with God is waiting to be recognized and expressed, direction can provide the place and climate for such growth. An example of how the interviewer discovers this is the dialogue that takes place between Cindy, a prospective directee, and Sam, the interviewer:

Cindy: As I said before, I really would like to pray, but I find it difficult and often end up wondering if it's of any use.

Sam: I hear you saying two things: that you'd like to pray and you keep trying, but you also wonder if it's of any use.

Cindy: That's right. Both things are true even though it probably seems strange to say that.

Sam: Is that something you'd want to explore with a spiritual director? That desire to pray, but the wondering about its value . . .

Cindy: Yes, perhaps the direction could give me an incentive, something to keep me going.

Sam: Why do you feel that you'd like to pray?

Cindy: I don't really know. Sometimes I say I'm not going to try anymore and feel OK about that, but then there's a kind of yearning or longing . . . some sense that God is waiting for me. Hmm . . . I don't think I've ever put it like that before.

Sam: So that even though you feel discouraged and make up your mind not to pray, there's a longing and a sense of God waiting that keeps coming back.

Cindy: Yes.

It will be useful at this point to look at another initial interview that takes up similar questions. We can then discuss the focus and intensity of the desire that appears in each of the two interviews.

Carole comes for an interview with Sam on the same day. After a few preliminary remarks she says something very similar to what Cindy said.

Carole: I'm finding daily prayer quite hard. I try to keep attentive but I get distracted easily. I'm tempted to just put prayer aside.

Sam: You try to pray every day, Carole, but you keep being distracted . . .

Carole: That's right, and I wonder sometimes why I bother.

Sam: Could you say something about how you feel spiritual direction could help you with this problem? Because it does sound as if there's a desire to pray, but also real frustration.

Carole: My hope would be that in talking with me about my prayer someone could help me to overcome the distractions.

Sam: Could you say a little more about that?

Carole: Well, I really want to pray . . .

Sam: You want to and I can hear that clearly. Maybe it would be useful if you could say something about why you want to. What do you think?

Carole: Why I want to pray? (Carole smiles and shrugs and then continues). I want to pray because I want to be a good Christian. Prayer should be part of my life. It's—it's the way I can find out what God wants of me.

In her talk with Sam, Cindy becomes more concrete about her desire. She began by stating her desire in general terms and expressing her frustration. Although the interviewer has learned no more about the difficulties she is encountering, both he and Cindy have learned something significant about her desire. They have noticed an intensity to her longing and a sense that God is waiting for her. Another person is involved in the relationship, and her focus is at least partly on that other person.

Carole, too, becomes more concrete. She wants to pray because she believes prayer will help her to discover what God wants of her. It is when she speaks of finding out what God wants that her intensity appears. Her focus is not so much on God as it is on what God wants.

Sam sees an admirable desire in each of these women. He also sees a difference in the focus of their desire and the point at which intensity appears. Both Cindy and Carole will probably be accepted for direction. The difference, however, will have consequences in the direction. Sam anticipates that it will take some time for Carole to recognize that God is not simply one who expects performance. God desires to be in fuller relationship with Carole.

2. Perseverance and Commitment

Another question has to do with perseverance. Desire has to be strong enough to carry with it a sense of commitment to continuing prayer.

We look for indications that prospective directees are ready to commit themselves to the tasks of praying and talking about what happens when they try to pray. In particular, we try to ascertain that applicants are not searching outside themselves for a method that will give them a permanent and short-cut answer to the problems of life and of God. Spiritual direction can look like another technique that will provide the right answer. We look for signs that prospective directees understand that relationship with God is an ongoing and continuous process. Spiritual direction can help a person to enter into and remain with the process. It is a journey of nights and days, of quiet cooling streams and roaring rivers. It contains its own particular and sometimes frightening joys and pains. The seeker has to understand this.

We gently point to a sense of perseverance, a willingness to plug away at prayer even when nothing seems to be happening, a commitment to the struggle that is part of any relationship, especially the relationship with God. This willingness to try, this willingness to work at and with the desire is a basic and essential ingredient of the applicant's readiness for direction. It makes spiritual direction a worthwhile process for both the directee and the director, to say nothing of its value to God.

It is not enough to assume that people will persevere. The signs of commitment should be concrete. For instance, when Priscilla tells Connie that she is looking forward to having a director who will assign scripture at their meetings, notice Connie's response:

Priscilla: I want to be accountable to someone. So I'm looking forward to getting scripture from my director and knowing that I have to report back on it.

Connie: You have a pretty definite image of how you'd like the spiritual director to be. I think, Priscilla, any director will be happy to suggest scripture passages from time to time, especially if one seems appropriate to what you've been talking about. And often when people are beginning to pray seriously, it can be a service for awhile to recommend several passages that could be used if they're helpful. Usually, however, we like to leave that up to you so that you get accustomed to using what seems best for you at the time you pray.

Connie is letting Priscilla know that this is *her* journey. Priscilla will be expected to take initiative and assume responsibility for her own growth. Priscilla is also learning about the role of the spiritual director. The director will help, encourage, support, and challenge, but will not take away Priscilla's freedom. Connie is also asking Priscilla whether she wants to begin the journey and persevere in the struggle to find her own way to God in prayer. Without initiative, personal responsibility, and growing freedom, there is little opportunity for perseverance to come into play.

Wally asks Liz in the course of his introductory interview about the time and frequency of direction:

Wally: I was thinking of coming for direction every three weeks or so. That would fit into my schedule. I'm going to be in the city every third Wednesday on business anyhow and could come over around 7:30 P.M.

Liz: That's something you'd have to take up with your director at your first visit. You'll have to check out your schedules together and see what's convenient for both of you. I would like to talk a bit about frequency of visits though, OK?

Wally: Of course.

Liz: How do you react to the idea of coming every week at the start of direction?

Wally: Why is coming every week so important?

Liz: First of all, it takes time to establish a good relationship with your director. It's seldom easy to talk about the deeper things in our lives, especially personal prayer. There's a time of testing and learning to trust.

If you come weekly in the beginning, it's easier for the trust level to build up more quickly.

Wally: It does make sense . . . but suppose nothing is happening? What do we talk about then?

Important information is being presented here. Liz is letting Wally know that there may be some inconvenience in his coming for direction. He cannot assume that his director will be available at the best time for him. Wally will have to ask himself if he is willing to take the trouble of juggling his schedule for the sake of direction.

Liz also tells Wally that establishing a relationship in which trust can grow takes time and effort. She lets Wally know that he will be expected to honor his commitment to pray and to talk about that prayer. His own question "But suppose nothing is happening?" reflects a dawning consciousness that coming for spiritual direction will not ensure that prayer will henceforth be easy. Coming in contact with these down-to-earth realities invites Wally to look more carefully at the strength of his commitment to direction.

Questions about the frequency and length of prayer evoke a response from the interviewer that can often surprise the prospective directee. This happens especially when guidelines and direct advice have been part of the applicant's expectation. Notice this conversation between Tina, an applicant, and Mary, who is interviewing her.

Tina: I was wondering about prayer time and what's expected here.

Mary: What would you mean by prayer time, Tina?

Tina: Well, if you want me to pray every day I know that I'd try, but my life is so hectic—and I never seem to be able to take more than half an hour when I do have time. You may not feel that's enough.

Mary: For the most part, Tina, you won't find your director asking you how often you pray, or when, or how long. What the director is going to be more interested in is what happened when you did pray, what it was like for you, and how you felt about what happened. What's important for us is that you keep trying to pray.

Tina: That's a relief. (Pause) But even as I say that, I'm wondering what will happen if I come in week after week and I haven't found time to pray.

Mary: You sound worried about that. Are you afraid that you won't find the time?

Tina: Not really. I'm feeling pretty determined right now. I think I just wanted to see how you might respond.

Mary: We would want to help you look at what's going on. Basically, your director would ask if you could go back and look again at the desire that brought you here.

Mary listens and asks questions that help Tina to focus her desire, but the decision to begin spiritual direction will be primarily hers. The clarity with which she chooses will help to determine the quality and effectiveness of the direction.

3. Ability to Interact

The ability to interact is vital to the development of growth in prayer. We look for the capacity to respond clearly and directly. Good interaction will also be a necessary component of direction. The interviewer's questions and comments should evoke answers that are intelligible to both people. If this happens, it can be assumed that a working relationship with the director and a developing relationship with God are likely to appear in the course of direction. If the interviewer knows what the person's desire is, there is some assurance that the prospective directee understands what spiritual direction involves.

To clarify what we mean by the ability to interact, we can glance at a few of the signs that indicate a *lack* of ability to interact well. One is incessant talking accompanied by aimless interior wandering. A simple question by the interviewer leads to a long, rambling, vague, yet highly detailed exposition of the person's life. The applicant never stays on target. The listener feels entangled in cobwebs or feels that he or she has been holding an open vessel that keeps overflowing. Often the person speaks in unfinished sentences accompanied by shrugs and thoughts that trail off aimlessly into a void.

Some people fall silent in an interview, and seem to be struggling. The interviewer sees the applicant shifting from one position to another, grimacing and showing other signs of stress. The words are few and far between. An interviewer must then find a way of helping the applicant to talk about what is happening if this is possible. Interviewers can find this hard to do, but usually it requires only a simple statement and a question. "You seem to be finding this interview somewhat difficult. Is there anything I can do to help you?" This often reduces tension and enables the person being interviewed to feel understood and supported.

It may be that the silence is caused by fear, caution, or confusion. Such feelings will usually be dissipated as the interview proceeds. If long, strained silences followed by terse, noncommittal answers continue throughout the interview, there should be considerable doubt in the interviewer's mind about the applicant's ability to interact easily and spontaneously. If the doubt is strong enough, but the interviewer has reason to think the applicant might be more articulate in a second interview, an opportunity for one should be suggested.

Sometimes the quality of a person's silence indicates that a great deal of thought, reflection or prayer is taking place in that person. An interviewer would recognize this and experience the silence as peaceful and productive. Much can be communicated without words.

Although it is useful to learn something about the person's background and life experience, the introductory interview is not designed to elicit a lot of facts. In a given interview, the interviewer may find that he or she has gathered a great deal of factual information, or little. But the success of the interview depends on what the interviewer and the applicant have learned about the applicant's motivation, commitment, and ability to interact. We have used examples that are pointed and will be clearly intelligible to the reader. We are aware that, in practice, what happens in the interview is not always as clear-cut and uncomplicated.

Applicants come with different life experiences, and each interview is unique. What many interviews have in common, however, is the interviewer's realization that the person is being invited by God to look at the possibility of a stronger relationship with God. It can be that a person is searching explicitly, not for a stronger relationship with God, but for more meaning to life. God is still relatively unfamiliar to the prospective directee, but the interviewer senses that this preliminary desire can well lead, in time, to wanting God to become more familiar.

Some People Are Not Drawn to Direction

There are many sincere religious people who live out their relationship with God without making use of spiritual direction. Bob is a lifelong Catholic and a practicing, dedicated charismatic. He values his prayer with his fellow charismatics and his relationship with God. His prayer keeps him fully satisfied. He does not experience any desire or longing for anything else. Spiritual direction is not a felt need in his life.

Living as good Christians is an important concern of many people who are not attracted to spiritual direction. They want to please God and to do whatever seems to be right. Occasionally they would like to talk about making decisions in accordance with God's will. They would like to be affirmed in this regard. To begin talking to God about what God is like seems strange and unappealing.

Some people too are interested in simply describing their prayer and religious experience. They want confirmation and may be looking for praise or discussion on an intellectual level. They would see no reason to discuss their personal relationship with God. They do not want to enter into this kind of faith dynamic, and what is most important, they do not feel drawn in this direction.

Some Seek Direction for the Wrong Reasons

There are also people who seek direction without an accurate idea of its focus and purpose.

Some have the impression that spiritual direction is a panacea for emotional difficulties. The religious atmosphere in which it takes place seems more attractive than the atmosphere in which secular services are offered. There are those who would benefit from counseling or psychotherapy but seek direction because it seems more acceptable. Trying to substitute spiritual direction for another discipline would not produce the results the person is looking for.

If someone is lacking in a basic sense of self, if someone has a deep and abiding anger stemming from some traumatic experience in childhood, the person's needs tend to be therapeutic and not spiritual. An alcoholic, for instance, cannot effectively use spiritual direction as a substitute for the help that can be given by Alcoholics Anonymous or a professional who is trained to help people cope with this addiction. Once the initial work has been completed and the person is experiencing at least partial success in dealing with his or her difficulties, spiritual direction becomes a possibility. Sometimes, however, a director may make a conscious decision to be a supportive and encouraging figure in such a person's struggle. It should be clear to both, though, that this support is not yet spiritual direction.

Some others who seek spiritual direction would be better served by attending workshops or taking courses that would provide them with at least a minimal theological or scriptural background. It is not the director's task to provide extensive theological knowledge or scriptural exegesis.

Sometimes, too, a person who asks for spiritual direction wants nothing more than the companionship of someone willing to engage in mutual conversation about faith. More often now than in the past this desire can be satisfied by groups that meet for faith sharing or for mutual encouragement on a basis of Christian friendship. Our attitude toward those who apply for direction has remained basically the same since the Center was established. We want to help them enter into the process most likely to further the growth the person desires. We have attempted to listen carefully to what the person says. We have tried to ask questions that would enable the person to recognize his or her basic desire and decide whether this desire could most readily be satisfied through spiritual direction. There can be a discrepancy between what the person wants at the moment and what the person more deeply desires. As people are assisted to become concrete and specific, they can begin to sense from within themselves the direction in which they genuinely want to go.

Seldom is a person who applies incapable of spiritual direction. Often enough, however, the person actually wants something else. If the person comes to realize this during the introductory interview, he or she is then more free to consider other options. If in the future the person decides to pursue spiritual direction, he or she can return to the center

People change. Prayer, sense of self, needs, attitudes, behavior, and values all change. Some of those who discover during an introductory interview that they are not ready for spiritual direction may come to realize a year or more later that they have become ready. Then they can experience a desire that is based on their readiness and on their understanding of what they want to give to direction as well as on their grasp of what they want to receive from it.

The Assessment

Because so much has been said and written about spiritual direction in the last 20 years, many people have become familiar with the shop language of direction. This enables some to be fluent about their desire for a deep relationship with God when they really are not prepared to allow such a relationship to come about. Their responses in an interview are both plausible and well-informed, and can lead both them and us to believe that they will indeed benefit from spiritual direction.

To protect the integrity of spiritual direction and even more important, to find out whether the directee is being genuinely helped, we ask each director to conduct with each directee an assessment of their work together. This assessment, which usually takes place after six or seven meetings, is not a surprise to directees. They have been told about it in the letter they received before their introductory interview, and it is usually mentioned during that interview itself.

Both director and directee need to be straightforward during the assessment. The desire for approval will make the raising of sensitive issues difficult for both. The director's tendency can be to gloss over behavior contrary to a directee's stated desire or hope. A directee may have spoken of a strong wish to pray frequently; yet in direction he or she has talked only of frustrations at the office and misunderstandings at home. These concerns have so pre-empted the direction sessions that prayer was scarcely mentioned. A director can allow this situation to continue far too long because he or she is afraid that pointing out what is happening will irritate the directee.

Some directees find it hard to slow down and become more reflective. Others are not aware of feelings that may be pushing them in a direction other than the one they desire. Some find it difficult to proceed with prayer because they are operating out of a sense of guilt, anger or fear. During the assessment, what can the director do? An example can help us here.

> *Martin*: We've spent a lot of time looking at your problems over these past several weeks. And that's been a help to you, I know.

> *Louise*: It's been years since I've been able to speak so freely to anyone about the things that bother me.

> *Martin*: I have wondered about your prayer, though. I remember that when you came you felt distant from God and wanted to establish a new relationship with God. Is that still a strong desire for you?
> (Louise was silent.)

> *Louise*: And I'm not doing that. Are you saying that I should just forget my problems and talk only about my prayer?

> *Martin*: Not at all, Louise. I do think, though, that we need to give more time to what's going on between yourself and God. How do you feel when I say that?

> *Louise*: I'm surprised. (A long pause here). I'm surprised because when you said what's going on between myself and God I immediately reacted.

> *Martin*: Can you say what happened?

> *Louise*: That's different from telling me I have to pray. It's different and it feels a bit shaky inside.

> *Martin*: That's very graphic, Louise. Shaky inside. Can you say more?

> *Louise*: I'm afraid, and I'm surprised at that. I'm also feeling there's something else going on. I'm starting to feel again that I do not want to be distant from God.

This conversation, gentle and straightforward, helps Louise to return to he initial desire for a closer relationship with God. We have reason to hope that Louise and Martin, working together, will eventually identify whatever it is that is making it hard for her to pray.

About the same time Martin has an assessment with Ray, who has been coming to see him weekly for about two months. Ray is rather taciturn and finds it difficult to talk about the things that bother him. Martin realizes this and wonders whether Ray will be able to point out aspects of the direction he has found less than helpful.

Martin: Have you had time, Ray, to think about spiritual direction as you have been experiencing it?

Ray: Yes, I have. I knew that it would be hard for me to do, so I spent a lot of time thinking about it. I even wrote some things down.

(Martin nods and Ray continues.)

Thinking of the ways you've been helpful was easy, but when I started trying to remember any ways you didn't help I was stuck. Then one thing jumped out at me.

(He pauses. Martin again nods for Ray to continue.)

Last week when I started trying to tell you about my prayer, you kept finishing all my sentences for me.

(Ray begins to get animated.)

I was trying to tell you how I was finding my prayer and before I could find the best word, you moved right in and said "frustrating." Actually, it hadn't been frustrating at all but I let it go. Now when I remember it I realize it made me angry. Do you get impatient with me?

We will leave Martin to deal with this question and look instead at what is happening within Ray. Here is a man who finds it difficult to talk about what bothers him. Yet in this assessment he finds the courage and the words to tell Martin what has bothered him and how it made him feel, and to ask Martin: "Do you get impatient with me?" Although Martin may have to deal with his own rueful feelings, let us hope he can find the grace to be pleased with Ray's growth and the part he has played in that growth. Now that Ray has freely told Martin that he made him angry and asked Martin how he feels about him, and has experienced Martin's acceptance, their relationship can grow.

Assessments should never be considered one-time-only experiences. Used appropriately, they enable the director and directee to sweep away doubts and misunderstandings that impede direction. They can also renew the directee's contact with the strength of the desire that brought the person to direction. For these reasons some directors now find periodic assessments a major help for their directees.

Ending Direction

Another result of assessment can be a decision to end direction. The decision can be made by the directee or the director. It is most satisfactory, however, when they come to it together.

Few prospects are as daunting as this for directors who have not yet experienced it. So directors often refrain from addressing this option, even when a directee is obviously not benefiting from direction. Every experienced director will recognize the avoidance implicit in the following statements. Directors say in supervision:

> I don't want him to feel I'm rejecting him. He's a nice person and he's been hurt enough already.

> When Fran first came, she said honestly that she didn't know whether she wanted to pray. Is she trying to pray? I don't think so, but I'd like to give her another month or two to see whether she can work things out.

> Dan does want to pray. He says he does and I believe him. But all he can think about right now is the divorce. So we're talking about that and building

a solid relationship. He'll be able to talk about God
and prayer when the divorce is settled.

These explanations are plausible. But a director must
also ask herself or himself questions like these: Am I afraid of
this person's anger? Am I avoiding a discussion because it
might be unpleasant for me? Is my need to be appreciated
preventing me from being direct? These questions should be
asked against the background of the director's responsibility
to do what she or he can to help a person to pray out of the
reality of the person's life.

A director's honesty will give him or her the freedom to
help a directee. It is far better to face an issue than to let a
directee believe that everything is well with the spiritual direction when it is not. It is easy to understand the director's
sympathy with the directee's difficulties, but eventually the
director's sympathy will give way to impatience. Then the directee will be perplexed without identifying the source of the
perplexity.

If, on the other hand, a spiritual director points in good
time to what he or she sees as a hindrance to direction, a
productive decision can be made. If directee and director decide to end direction, they can then consider other options that
would enable the directee to pursue the growth he or she desires.

An incident that took place several years ago illustrates
the positive results that ending direction can have. Paul came
to be interviewed for direction. At the end of his introductory
interview, he was accepted for direction. He then mentioned
that he had been at the Center nine years before. His direction at that time ended after a few months.

Paul said:

As I look back now, I see how surly I was. I could
not believe in God so I couldn't pray. I challenged
my director to prove that God existed, and when she
replied, I fought her every inch of the way. When
she finally suggested that counseling might be more

helpful than spiritual direction, I told her that if she were a good director she could help me herself. She remained kind and firm until the end of our visit. I was surprised when she suggested I think about what she had said and come back the next week. I never did return.

Paul continued:
I wish I could tell her now how grateful I am for her honesty. I did finally end up in therapy. I had some discoveries to make before I could even begin to think about praying. Now I know two things: God was waiting for me all that time and loving me too. And that director loved me enough to tell me the truth, and start me on the road to emotional and spiritual health.

We can see how painful the discussion that concluded direction was for both the director and Paul. We hope it is also obvious that it was less painful than continuing a process that could delay the directee's discovery of a freeing and enabling alternative.

Some directees have been surprised, almost incredulous, to hear directees praising them for qualities they never knew they had.

Don: I've done reviews with six directees over the past two weeks, and four of them spoke first about my sensitivity and gentleness.

Supervisor: You seem surprised, Don.

Don: I've spent most of my life feeling like a bull in a china shop . . . big, awkward, always in the way.

Supervisor: And now you're finding that others don't see you that way.

Don: It's going to take a while to absorb that. But I have to pay attention, especially because they all had very specific situations to point at.

Supervisor: What's it doing to your sense of yourself as a director?

Don: I cried a little bit a couple of times this week. I felt so much lighter and more confident.

Other directors may feel that they talk too much, or too little, and can be startled to find that their directees experience them as offering just the right amount of conversation for helpful dialogue.

Many directors are encouraged when directees affirm strengths they have already recognized in themselves before. Ellen tells her supervisor a typical story:

I've always felt that I had a real ability to challenge people without being threatening. But you know I can wonder about that too, wonder if I'm really as helpful in situations as I credit myself with being. Hearing that quality affirmed in me is a source of peace and strength for my ministry.

Directors need to hear about their strengths and how productive these can be in a directee's growth. This provides a confirmation for them that cannot be experienced in any other way. It gives them a sense of stability and a sureness about themselves as directors.

Another related purpose is to find out what the director does that is least helpful. It can be that the directee finds it "least helpful" because it is challenging and thus somewhat fearful. Often, however, a director finds that the directee is picking up and reacting to a habit, attitude, or quality that does indeed impede or retard the onward flow of the direction.

Some directors have an irritating habit of finishing a directee's comments. Alice may say: "After not being able to pray for a week, I'm feeling" . . . and Chris moves right in to say ". . . frustrated." Whether or not this is the correct feeling is irrelevant. What Chris has done is to interrupt the process of self-discovery.

The list of "least helpfuls" is endless, and a director feels at least as vulnerable during this part of the review as does the directee. Any sense of being "in charge" has to be given up, at least temporarily. The anxieties of the director can be disquieting, but can also sharpen the director's awareness, and this is always productive.

A well-done review is a source of both satisfaction and chagrin to a director.

Ruth: The way you can sit and be silent when I'm finding it hard to talk helps me to relax and let the words come—so that I'm not trying to monitor my every word, for fear of how it will sound.

Clara: I'm glad to hear that. I've found myself that your silences are powerful prayer. Was there anything else you wanted to say?

Ruth: Yes, but this is more difficult. (Long pause) I believe you really do want me to tell you anything that's bothering me.

Clara: Yes, I do because it will help our future sessions together.

Ruth: Sometimes you tell me how well I'm doing, especially at the end of a session when I haven't done well at all. I get annoyed because I need you to help me to look at that squarely. When you try to make me feel good about myself instead, it's as though I were a child getting patted on the head.

Clara: (Grimacing, but nodding her head) Okay. I've been so aware of how hard this process has been for you that I've paid too much attention to encouraging you and end up making you feel like a child. I need to let both of us trust the courage that keeps you going— am I catching what you're telling me?

Ruth: That's right! That's how it feels , and I need to know you recognize that. You've helped me a lot and

I'm grateful. (Sitting back with a sigh) Well, now it's your turn.

If Clara felt threatened before, she may well find that the prospect of telling Ruth what she needs to hear is capable of arousing even deeper feelings in her.

The Director's Experience

A director needs to develop the ability to be straightforward with directees. Nothing militates against these qualities as much as the universal need to be liked and to be approved. This need for approval will sometimes make it difficult for a director to raise an issue which needs attention. The review offers that opportunity. We look now at one example of how the director does this:

Shirley: I'd like to begin my part of the review by telling you that I've often felt privileged to be part of your journey. We've been up on some high mountains and deep into a few jungles. I have admired your persistence, your determination to find God for yourself.

Joel: I'm grateful for those words, Shirley, and aware of how often I would have given up without your support.

Shirley: That's OK, Joel, but I'm curious to know if you can accept what I've seen as your strength.

Joel: It's hard but I am beginning to see that I do have a lot of determination.

Shirley: I also see a strong desire to know God personally, to let God be more a part of your everyday life.

Joel nods and sits quietly. After a few minutes—

Shirley: I have noticed another pattern, Joel. You can be faithful to spiritual direction as long as we're on a mountain or lost in the jungle, but you find it hard to deal with plodding.

Joel: Plodding?

Shirley: Yes, when prayer is a little tedious, even boring, have you noticed that's when you're most likely to start coming late, leaving early, canceling at the last minute?

Joel: (long pause) I feel chagrined, even a little angry to hear you say that—but I know it's true.

Shirley: I'm bringing it up, Joel, not because I want to blame you but because God may often be with you in the boredom and you need to pay attention.

Joel: OK, I never thought of that. I would just feel I needed to escape, to stop talking when there wasn't anything to talk about.

Shirley and Joel agree to take some time before their next meeting to reflect on what has happened and, in particular, to look squarely at the tedious, boring times in prayer. Both leave the review conscious that they have taken a step forward together. The review has done its work.

Termination

One result of the review is a step toward growth. Another is a more candid relationship between a director and directee. Yet another result can be termination. A director can hesitate even when the directee is obviously looking for something other than spiritual direction. Directors will say:

I don't want to hurt Len. He's an awfully nice person and he's been hurt enough already.

When Fran first came, she was very honest about saying she didn't know if she wanted to pray. I'd like to give her a few more months to work things out.

Dan does want to pray. He says it and I believe him. I think I'm doing the right thing by supporting him as he works through his divorce and settlement. Maybe later, he'll be ready to pray and we'll have a good relationship already established.

We have sympathy for these various attitudes and feelings. But experience teaches us that a director can begin to build up feelings of resentment when time passes and directees who were not praying after seven weeks are still not praying after seven months. Sympathy is replaced by anger, patience becomes impatience. The directee is not to be faulted for this. It is the director who failed to help the directee look at the spiritual direction relationship and see that something important was missing—the ability to pray at this point in the directee's life.

Termination need not be experienced as total failure on the directee's part. If the interviewer has been careful and clear with the applicant, both are able to look at the process of beginning spiritual direction as discovery.

The first several visits serve to answer these major questions: Does this process help me to come to know God in a more intimate way? Or, am I coming to see that some other way may be more productive for me at this time? If so, how can my spiritual director help me determine the next step in my search?

It is an undeniable fact that some people, both directors and directees, find termination painful. It will be less painful, however, than continuing a process which is not helpful and which delays discovery of the discipline that is enabling and freeing for the directee.

Chapter 4

The Spiritual Director: Motivation and Experience

Introduction

In Chapter 3 we spoke of the people who have come to the center for spiritual direction, and of the hopes that brought them. In this chapter we give our attention to the spiritual directors who help them.

At the Center we have had an extraordinary large number of opportunities to work with spiritual directors. More than 150 people have participated in the nine-month program we conduct in Cambridge for the further development of directors. Another 120 directors have participated in 10-week programs we have offered in Australia and New Zealand. We have also conducted numerous shorter programs throughout the United States, Canada, and Ireland. Most of those who participated in the programs we have given were experienced directors before they began their work with us.

What have these women and men been like and what has attracted them to the ministry of spiritual direction? Is there anything about a person's life experience and personal history that clearly points toward an attraction initiated by God? We address these questions in the context in which we have most often had occasion to raise them: the process through which we decide on applications to the associates' program. This is a program in which experienced directors work alongside the staff for most of a year in order to further develop their ability as directors. Admission to the program takes place after a series of communications which culminate in a personal interview. In the course of the application process we try to find out what the applicant is like, what attracted him or her to the ministry of direction, and whether he or she is likely to benefit from participation in the program.

The Personal Interview

Like the administrators of other ministerial programs, we ask applicants for the usual documents that give information about their life and experience: educational records, references, an autobiographical sketch, and other background information. We also ask for a description of the person's experience of giving spiritual direction.

It is the personal interview with the full-time staff, however, that is most consistently charged with life for ourselves and for the applicants. Two aspects of the interview contribute to this vitality. All full-time staff members (there were four in 1993-1994) take part and work together toward a consensus. Applicants thus have an opportunity to observe the interaction that will be characteristic of staff work during the program. The entire staff also interact with the applicant, an arrangement that allows the applicant to estimate how he or she might react to them during the year. Because our work with associates tends to be close and personal, we want to give applicants a fair opportunity to see us in action so that they can decide whether they are likely to feel at home at the center.

Decisions on applicants are based on objective qualifications, but there is an intangible aspect too. We look for a clear, specific description of the person's desire to pursue this ministry. The staff invests a great deal of time, thought, and energy in the development of each associate. We have said to one another, only partly in jest, "We are married to them for the year." It is important for us to know how they plan to use what they receive and how well the program fits their experience, needs, and desires. We look at these issues in detail when we speak of the questions asked in the interview. First, however, we will direct our attention to a few of the more significant qualities we consider fundamental in prospective associate directors.

Age and Life Experience

Advancing years can be a decided asset for spiritual directors, provided the directors have learned through their experience. Life contains a variety of faulty beginnings and unresolved endings. It brings us broken relationships and the untimely loss of people we love. Life also brings us sustained and sustaining friendships, and times of creativity and fulfillment. The rebirth of nature, and the arrival of the long awaited infant proclaim the splendor of life and ask us to pay attention, to respond, and to continue searching. If we listen to life as it unfolds, we come to know that its adventure lies in the search rather than in the expectation of clear and concrete answers. It is the attractiveness of the search that moves us forward. We learn the hard-won lesson of gentle patience with ourselves and others. The fire still burns but it burns now in brightly glowing embers.

This is what we mean:

Initially, Colin was cautious in stating his qualifications for the program. He said:

> My age—I'm 65—makes me hesitate to apply, even though my provincial has urged me to do it, and so have several of my colleagues.

He paused, and then went on:

> There was a time when I had all the answers. I know no other way of being productive. Then, in my mid-50's I contracted a serious infection that clouded my vision. It forced me to depend on others for almost a year. I bitterly resented my dependence. A priest friend of mine used to stop by every

day at meal time and check over my food and cut my meat. I was grateful but it was galling to be so helpless. One day he said how life-giving it was for him to be able to help me. I had always seemed so strong before that there was nothing he could do for me. That simple statement of his changed me and led me here. My eyes were still giving me a lot of trouble, but inwardly I began to see in ways I'd never seen before. I've learned to enjoy helping other people to discover the gifts they haven't recognized they have. I've been fairly successful at it. I figure that I have a good ten or even fifteen years left to me and with the help I can get here I think I would be even more successful.

Personal Maturity

The desire to listen to another person's experience of God and of life is indispensable for a spiritual director. Is it enough, however, to make a person a genuinely helpful director? We have learned to look for several characteristics of personal maturity that we believe must accompany this desire.

We want to know, first of all, whether the person has enough independence of mind to learn from other people and yet come to convictions that will be distinctively the person's own. In the associates' program the other people will be primarily the person's directees, the staff, and the other associates. Relatively mature associates will learn from directees and allow the views of staff members and other colleagues to modify or confirm their own. They will not, however, rely exclusively on what Joe or Mary says, or lapse into helpless bewilderment when, in a consultation, staff members disagree with one another.

There are other aspects of maturity too that will have marked influence on an associate's direction. The work of direction is frequently slow, and its most important results often appear only gradually. To remain engaged and yet respect the directee's freedom requires a strong sense of responsibility. At the same time, directors have to maintain enough balance to avoid taking on other responsibilities that belong to the directee, not to them. Directors have a responsibility to help directees with their relationship with God. When they also imagine themselves responsible for the relationship itself, or for the directee's health or marital happiness, for example, they run a risk of both overtaxing themselves and making the helping relationship between director and directee the focus of the direction, rather than the directee's relationship with God. When this happens, the relationship with God receives little attention.

In considering prospective associates, then, we have to determine whether they will be able both to commit themselves to helping others and also to give themselves to the task of facilitating the relationship between directees and God. If they themselves have had experience of life and of God, they have encountered some of the pitfalls that can entrap people who want to pursue that relationship. In their ministry of spiritual direction, too, they have encountered those pitfalls. If they have learned from their experience, they know that one can avoid them or, if one is unfortunate enough to fall into the pit, can climb out or be drawn out again.

Mature applicants have also experienced the joys and rewards that life holds for those who try to do what seems right without evading responsibility. They have experienced what it is like to love and to be loved, to care for another and let themselves be cared for. They have touched the richness of God's love in them and for them. This has strengthened their commitment and strengthened their desire for others to experience the love they have experienced. They do not give up easily. They know that God's love can be counted on. They have resources of trust within themselves that enable them to believe that God will reveal Godself to the directee.

In her application interview, Kay says:

I was always in awe of the way some people kept praying, even when nothing seemed to be happening between themselves and God. I felt that the least I could do was to keep encouraging them, even though I often felt discouraged myself.

I recall vividly how a directee came in one day, buoyant and lighthearted. It was easy to see that something wonderful had occurred. She told me about an experience of God's love in prayer that, as she described it, moved us both to tears. But the most profound impact came when she said how grateful she was to me. She had kept searching, she said, because of my attitude of trust. That was a revelation for me. I saw for the first time that, even beneath the discouragement I sometimes felt, I had an abiding trust in the God who had always been there for me and would always be there for others. I could sense God nodding, and I knew then how deep my own commitment really was.

Receptivity

We look for freedom and an open attitude toward life and people. Mature religious people understand that their journey belongs to them and has its own peculiar characteristics. They do not expect a directee to follow their paths or to have their values. They understand that each person's relationship with God has its own distinct quality. Their receptivity to others enables them to dismiss any expectation that a directee's journey with God will be a carbon copy of their own.

An applicant tells this story about himself:

When I began to do direction I found myself frustrated and anxious. I never felt satisfied with what was happening to my directees. This all came to a head for me one day when Joan, one of my directees, got really angry with me. She had sensed God coming close in prayer, and she had also noticed that I was skeptical when she tried to tell me about it. Lucky for me that she thought enough of our relationship to fight about it. As we talked I could see that I was measuring her experience against my own and not valuing it. My direction changed immediately. I found I could let other people be different, and as I let this happen, my frustration disappeared. Now I find myself almost overwhelmed at times with the variety of ways in which God approaches. It's never the same. Every person is unique to God, and God is unique to every person.

Receptivity does not mean agreeing with all of a directee's beliefs and values or accepting all a directee's aspirations. Directee and director will not have identical attitudes toward every issue. Directors even have to expect that their sense of moral or spiritual rightness will be offended by some of the beliefs, actions, and aspirations they encounter in direction. When that happens they will have to be sure they are aware of their feelings and keep in mind that their responsibility requires, not that they try to change the directee's attitudes, but that they help the person to communicate frankly with God.

They have to trust God to reveal Godself to the directee. And they have to trust that this self-disclosure on God's part will effect any changes that need to be made.

Like the other attitudes we have described, receptivity may not be fully developed in a prospective director, but it is vitally important that its basic lineaments be present; otherwise, the candidate cannot be fully available for the spiritual service of others.

What Happens in the Application Interview?

The staff come to application interviews with several purposes in mind. One of these purposes has to do with the applicants' ability to give spiritual direction. We ask ourselves: Are these applicants likely to become more capable directors through participation in the program, and are the directees they will see likely to benefit from ministry?

We also want to know whether ours is the most suitable program for particular applicants and, if it is, whether this is the right time for them to enter it. So we ask ourselves: Would these applicants be better served by a program with different emphases? Or we may wonder: Would they be more able directors in the long run if they waited a year longer before entering the program?

We also want to decide whether an applicant is likely to get along with the staff and other applicants who will enter the program that year.

The format of the interview is flexible. The staff has no set of questions that must be answered. There are, however, topics that must be explored if applicants and staff are to reach a mutual agreement on what the person needs and expects and whether the associates' program is likely to meet those needs and expectations.

THE MAJOR TOPICS

One of the interviewers may begin with this question: "Could you tell us what led you to decide on spiritual direction as a ministry?" We want to hear what brought the person originally to take up the ministry of spiritual direction and what persuaded him or her to continue in it. Here is a representative reply:

Eleanor: I had been teaching happily for about 25 years and never thought about doing anything else. One day another teacher stopped by after class and we began to talk about her prayer. As she was leaving, she asked me if I had ever thought of becoming a spiritual director. I was speechless at the very idea! But later, when I reflected on it, I could see how many of my colleagues, students, and even parents, had been coming to me for a long time. They would talk about their problems, but also they talked about their prayer and God. The longer I reflected, the more I realized that I had seen some of these people's lives change for the better. They came closer to God, and became more patient, and more understanding of others.

I could go on and on, but the last thing I want to share with you is the sense of confidence I've felt since then, and a growing trust that I'm not alone. I believe that God is somehow with me in that ministry.

Other applicants describe similar happenings. Some, engaged in parish ministries, find themselves being approached by others and responding to requests for help with prayer and relationship with God. Their initial reaction is often tentative, but they grow in confidence as they see positive results. They also begin to trust that God is helping them. We see this happening not only to members of religious congregations but also to married or single women and men in increasing numbers.

Joe, a brother in a religious community, tells us:

I've been part of a team assigned to train young brothers. Other members of the team told me they avoided talking about prayer because the young brothers never seemed to know what to say. That surprised me. I found some of them came to me on their own to talk about getting closer to God. I like doing this and I feel drawn to doing it more often.

In these two examples, and in many others, we see clear indications that the person is being called to this particular ministry by people with whom he or she associates. That a person finds the ministry attractive can be a sound reason to consider engaging in it. Being invited by others to engage in it is, however, a more cogent reason. Still more powerful is evidence of the director's developing reliance on God's presence and aid.

To make a knowledgeable decision about each applicant, we need to know approximately how many people an applicant has directed and whether the direction has been long-term or of short duration. It helps us to know if the directees have come from a variety of life experiences, occupations, and church affiliations, if any.

Basically, however, we listen for more than facts, important as these are. As a person speaks of his of her experience, we also listen for them to say something that will indicate their ability to reflect on each person's experience. We want to hear that the applicant has seen development in a directee's prayer and spiritual life.

If applicants do not mention their personal prayer in the course of discussion, we ask them about it. "Prayer" has such different meanings for different people that we often have to ask—though we do so apologetically—what the person's prayer is like.

We hope to learn answers to these questions: Does the applicant have a relationship with God that he or she can describe to some extent? Can the applicant speak about his or her own religious experience, times when the person was aware that God was acting in and with him or her? Does the person show some awareness of his or her own desires in prayer and the ways in which he or she resists prayer as well? Has the person learned how to communicate his or her life, feelings, doubts and boredom, delights and enthusiasms to God? Without some of this deeply personal experience, a director would find it difficult to empathize with a directee's experience as he or she tried to pray.

It is not easy for an applicant to describe experiences of God to comparative strangers. Realizing that, we do not ask for detailed descriptions. However, in order to estimate intelligently an applicant's ability to give direction, we have to hear more specific descriptions than:

God is a Presence.

or

My prayer has always been good.

When applicants return only vague answers, one of us is likely to say: "We realize that it's difficult to speak more concretely about this in an interview. But we wonder whether there is an example you could give of how you have experienced God in prayer. We are not looking for anything dramatic. Maybe there is an experience from a retreat you have made, some concrete experience from your last retreat, for instance. We're looking for some sense of the way you relate to God and God relates to you."

A serious question can arise if applicants are unable to say anything specific about their experience of prayer. A remark like "I find it easy to pray on retreat and feel that God is pleased" tells us something, but not much. The difference is evident when an applicant replies:

> My last retreat experience was difficult, yet it was satisfying too. At the beginning God seemed very distant, and I could not pray. I finally got a little desperate and found myself telling God how I felt. It seemed to me that I heard him saying, 'You're trying too hard. I'm here. Just relax and let me do some of the work.' It was as though a burden was being lifted from my shoulders. There were no dramatic experiences after that, but during the rest of the retreat, I found myself talking to him spontaneously. He seemed to be pleased with me. It was almost as though, if I could see God, he would be smiling, nodding his head, encouraging me.

In this instance the person is able to be frank with God about her feelings. She senses a response from God, and she experiences a change in herself and in her relationship with God. The applicant can describe God in personal terms rather than in general statements. She tells us something about the way she focuses in her prayer. We know at once that this person shows promise of recognizing the value of helping another person to interact with God.

Why Choose this Program?

Many applicants have attended workshops given by the staff. Others have read some of the writings of staff members. Those who have become acquainted with our work in one of these ways have usually reflected on what they have heard or read and have concluded that spiritual direction as we practice it can open the way for something life-giving to happen between a person and God. Some are particularly attracted by the fact that in this direction prayer focuses on what God is like and what God is doing. They may also be attracted by the fact that directees are often encouraged to enter a "dialogue" with God. Whatever the details of the applicant's reply might be, we want to know whether he or she sees enough that is distinctive about the program to justify giving the necessary time, initiative, and energy to it.

The most experienced applicants often single out the opportunity to have their work supervised frequently and regularly as the component of the program that appeals most to them. Often these applicants have had training in spiritual direction. They say:

> I had some excellent courses and workshops during my previous training as a director. In looking back, however, I realize that I always wanted something else. It's taken me a while to recognize that I was feeling a need to have objective feedback on my ministry. I am looking forward to both affirmation and challenge on the quality of my direction this year.

Another applicant might remark:

> I did get some supervision in my previous program. I found it both helpful and frustrating. I learned from the supervision, but it was too sporadic. There just wasn't enough of it to make a strong, lasting impression on my direction.

Applicants express their attraction to another prominent aspect of the program by saying:

I already have all the degrees I believe I need for my work as a spiritual director. What I don't have is the give and take of working with, and getting critiqued by, a group of my peers as well as a staff. I know that might prove hard for me to accept, but I'm looking forward to the experience.

The Applicant's Awareness of Doubts and Fears

When applicants arrive for the interview they are usually prepared to offer us cogent reasons for accepting them into the program. We want to hear those reasons because we are interested in an applicant's appraisal of her or his capabilities. It is just as important, however, for us to hear indications that an applicant is aware of fears, anxieties, or doubts. If an applicant seems unaware that the program is demanding, or appears unwilling to accept the fact that it may at times arouse fear and self-doubt, the staff tries to determine the source of this composure. Does it stem from the person's desire to appear appropriately self-confident or from a lack of self-knowledge? Thus an exchange like this might occur:

Jerry (one of the staff): You've told us a great deal about your desire to develop further as a spiritual director. You've had a lot of experience and you have a fine background in theology and counseling. It's an impressive picture. Could you tell us about any doubts or fears you might have, or any difficulties you're aware of that could get in the way of your becoming an even better director?

Bob (an applicant): I suppose there's some anxiety about being accepted. I do think I have the qualifications, but I know that you take only a limited number of people. If you don't accept me I'll be disappointed . . .

Jerry: That would be the only feeling? Anxiety about not being accepted because of our limited numbers?

Bob: Yes. I can't think of anything else.

Suppose that, instead of replying as he did, Bob said:

> Doubts and difficulties? Well, I'm not sure how ef-
> fective I can be with people who say they want to
> pray but don't, and with people who have a lot of
> difficulty getting started with prayer. I get tense
> and start talking too much. I feel as though I
> should be able to solve their problem. Then I get
> impatient, too. I want people to move faster than
> they can. I know they pick up my tension some-
> times, and that just adds to their distress. That's
> what I'm most aware of right now: I'm unsure there.

Our first version of Bob's reply would leave us wondering
whether he was reflective enough to doubt and perceptive
enough to recognize difficulties he might have as a director.
We would also question his sensitivity to his feelings. Without these resources he would find it difficult, if not impossible,
to develop interiorly and ground the quality of his direction on
experience rather than techniques.

The second version is vastly different. Bob shows himself aware of difficulties he has as a director. He states the
circumstances in which those difficulties arise, and by describing his tension and excessive talking, he discloses his concrete
physical and psychological reactions to these circumstances.
Bob thus gives clear indications that he will be a perceptive
and candid participant in supervision. Despite the difficulties
he has indicated, he is a promising candidate for the program.

The Applicant's Hopes for the Future

At some point in the interview, if the subject has not yet
been discussed, one of the staff will ask: What do you want to
do in ministry after completing the associates' program? Any
hopes? Any dreams?

One of the purposes of the application interview is to determine whether the applicant is likely to make use of his or her experience at the Center to give direction after he or she leaves us. Credentials are important to ministerial careers, and we sympathize with applicants' need of them. But we prefer applicants who can indicate that after they leave the Center they will devote a substantial amount of time to giving spiritual direction. We know, of course, that some graduates will soon be busy with tasks other than direction. We try to determine, however, whether they will also have opportunities to continue to give direction in the next few years. The associates' program fulfills its basic purpose only when graduates are helping people develop their relationship with God.

We also have desires and dreams for the development of the ministry. As we listen to applicants we ask ourselves whether they show promise of developing new ideas or of eventually launching new enterprises.

We give some preference to those who seem capable of initiating new enterprises. We also give preference to those whose background indicates they might write about spirituality from the point of view of what happens in people's prayer.

Some applicants have had experience of working with underprivileged people, with minority groups, or in some other area where social need is prominent. Some know that they will return to places in the world where it is impossible to receive spiritual direction. We also give preference to them.

Since the mid-1970s when two graduates of the associates' program, assisted by one of the Center staff, established the Jamaican Center for Religious Development, the Center has been influenced by the pastoral needs of the Third World. Graduates have worked as spiritual directors and in the organization of spiritual direction programs in the West Indies, Latin America, New Guinea, and Africa. Now, as the 1990s advance, it is a rare year when at least one person working in one of those regions does not apply for admission to the associates' program. We have been eager to accommodate these applicants; indeed, it has been our hope since the planning of the Jamaican venture that spiritual direction, with its emphasis on a person's own experience of God, which takes place within the person's cultural context, could contribute significantly to the growth of indigenous spiritual life in cultures very different from our own.

Outcome of the Interview

Although we do not formally accept an applicant at the end of an application interview, we are careful to give the person a clear indication of the likelihood of his or her acceptance. The person may be told that he or she is a strong or adequate candidate. If the staff doubt the person's suitability or readiness for the program, they say this to the applicant. If for some reason the applicant looks as though he or she would not benefit significantly from the program, we say this and we also point out the strengths we have noticed in the person's abilities and background. Often we can suggest alternative programs that would be better attuned to the person's needs than ours would be, a way of getting more experience before committing himself or herself to a demanding ministerial program, or another area of ministry that would be better suited to his or her talents or expectations. These suggestions, given by a group of experienced ministers after the intensive discussion characteristic of these interviews, often prove valuable to the applicant.

Since physical accommodations at the Center are limited, and the time available for supervision is more restricted in some years than in others, we sometimes ask qualified candidates to wait for a year. When we foresee that this may happen, we inform applicants of this possibility so that they will have an opportunity to make other plans. When it does happen, and the candidate chooses to apply again the following year, we do not require another interview and we give the person preferred standing among the applicants for that year.

There are occasions, too, when the coming year may not be the right time in an applicant's life to enter the program. An applicant may have just been married, for example, or be preparing for ordination or for final commitment in a religious congregation, and so may be too emotionally preoccupied for the time being to take on another venture that would make heavy demands on his or her inner resources.

. Other applicants may have just completed years, sometimes many years, in a responsible and arduous ministry—the presidency of a university, for example, or a major administrative position in a religious congregation. They have sabbatical time at their disposal, but the combination of the change in ministry and the tempo of the program may prove too much for them to cope with gracefully. We often recommend to such applicants that they spend a year in an occupation that will allow them a more regular schedule. If they have held positions of considerable authority, the year should also offer them an opportunity to associate with more people on a peer level.

We have discussed the decision-making that takes place during the application interview primarily from the staff's point of view. Applicants, however, also have decisions to make. Now that they have met the staff and discussed the program and their application with them, they have to ask themselves whether this program is likely to help them get what they were looking for when they applied. They also have to ask themselves: Do I want to spend a year with these people? Finally, they have to decide in light of the discussion whether this is the right time for them to enter on such a program.

Usually the interview confirms decisions the applicant has already made. This is not always true, however. Sometimes an applicant finds, for instance, that the program's concentration on spiritual direction is more exclusive than he or she expected, and decides that it would leave too little time for other interests he or she intends to pursue during the year. Sometimes, too, an applicant doubts whether he or she has enough theological background to be fully at home in the program. When a person whose application seems acceptable to the staff remains uncertain at the end of the interview, the staff suggest that he or she take time to consider further and then inform us of the decision that emerges from this consideration.

The Final Selection of Candidates

The Center's application process, from the arrival of the initial request for information to the final decision on the person's application, is designed to enable the staff to select for the program the individuals who are likely to benefit most from it.

In addition, the staff also pays attention to the composition of the group. There is a decided advantage, for one thing, to having a group made up of roughly equal numbers of women and men. Men and women have much to learn from one another in a situation of shared ministry. Consideration is also given to the age level of the group. When the group includes people of different ages, from the later 30s to the later 60s, communication develops that enables its members to pass beyond fixed concepts about the values and attitudes of generations other than their own. As they share their lives and their current ministerial experience, they also come to recognize what they can give to each other and how much encouragement and support they can receive from one another. Whenever lay people are members of this group, whenever Protestant ministers participate in the program, whenever people from other countries enter into this experience at the center, the educative potential of the group is increased.

Our admissions procedures are not perfect. Despite our efforts, we have accepted applicants who have not benefited from the program as we hoped they would. Nor have all groups done as much as we would wish to bring about a collaborative working environment. As we look back over the years since 1972, however, we believe the associates' program has for the most part accomplished what it was designed to do, and that its success owes much to our admissions procedures. We have learned from our experience where some of those procedures have required correction and development, and have tried to provide them. We expect to learn more.

Chapter 5

Development of the Director's Faith as a Basis for Ministry

One of the convictions that led to the establishment of the Center was the belief that the day of the lone wolf spiritual director, who did his or her work while associating seldom with other directors, was over. Once directors began to ask "What happens when you try to pray?"—instead of "Do you pray?"— and waited for the directee to reply, they began to walk in a world of experience that had previously been closed to them. To find their way in that world and not grow laggard in their exploration of it, they needed support from other directors who had entered it. For the first staff, the opportunity to talk frequently about their ministry with colleagues who had embarked on the same exploration was one of the most exhilarating features of their association with the Center.

When the first associates joined us, we hoped they would experience the same kind of working and exploring fellowship that sustained and inspirited us. We hoped they would experience it among themselves and with the staff during their time at the Center, and that this experience would encourage them to seek similar experiences of fellowship in their later ministry. We learned, however, that such an experience does not occur readily. It requires time and opportunity. It also requires the development of the associates' ability to disclose themselves to others and to listen as others disclose themselves to them.

The First Seabrook Meeting

The work of establishing a basis of trust on which fellowship can develop begins when the new associates arrive in early September to begin their year of work at the Center. Within a few weeks of their arrival all of us—associates and permanent staff—take ourselves for three days to a house at Seabrook Beach on the New Hampshire coast to lay a common foundation for the work and reflection of the year.

The permanent staff have two specific hopes for this meeting: that we come to know one another and that we come to describe to one another something of our personal experience of God, to the extent that each person can and chooses to describe that experience. The atmosphere is one of freedom. The house, casual and pleasant, with a spacious living room looking through a picture window across dunes to the sea, breathes freedom and relaxation. The time-arrangement is relaxed and flexible, with the greater part of each day left free for people to do with it what they please: talk together, walk on the shore, swim, play billiards, make sorties to nearby discount stores, watch television. Whatever specific activity or non-activity they choose, much of the time is devoted to the informal business of coming to know one another.

Arrangements for the sessions in which we invite the group to describe to one another something of their experience of God we try to keep in harmony with this informal atmosphere. No one has to speak at any of the sessions, and participants are repeatedly reminded that, although anything they say will contribute to the value of the group experience, we hope they will keep in mind that they are free to say as much or as little as they choose.

Concern for Freedom

Why be so careful about freedom? First of all, because the awareness of what happens in people's hearts gives a spiritual director a profound regard for people's freedom. Little seems to happen between God and a person without the person's freedom being involved. Although much of what God gives us is given unasked, it is only with freedom that a person accepts what God gives precisely as a gift. Unless a person freely accepts, the giving does not have the significance for the conscious relationship with God that it can have. We have eyes and can see with them, but unless we freely accept them as a gift of God, the fact that we have them is not a strand in the conscious bond between ourselves and God.

The crucial part that our freedom plays in our conscious relationship with God is borne in on us so often that whenever we talk about prayer, we try to keep people aware of this freedom. Awareness of this freedom can easily be submerged in the pursuance of a program. During the year we are beginning, we want to keep it in full view.

A keen awareness of our freedom is especially pertinent to the sessions at Seabrook, for we are invited during these sessions to describe to one another experiences that have to do with our relationship with God. No other relationship is as intimate as our relationship with God, and no one and no program has the right to require us to disclose experiences that reveal it. Since their ministry cannot be effectively pursued without exploration of directees' religious experience, it is important that associates have some ability to disclose their own experience. If they do not, it will be difficult for them to help directees to disclose theirs. Nevertheless, it would still not be right to require such disclosures of the associates. If they are to be made, they have to be made freely.

Do we run a risk of fostering a degree of exhibitionism when we invite one another to speak of our religious experience? Viewed in abstraction from the actual situation that obtains at the Seabrook meeting, this could be a reasonable concern. What better way can there be of inspiring admiration in a group of spiritual directors than recounting one's experiences of God? In the actual situation, however, there is less reason for concern. For most associates, "faith sharing" with a group has not in recent years been a new experience. Most associates have already experienced it in prayer groups or discernment meetings. Then, too, the staff make clear as the meeting begins that talking on this level has a clear purpose: it is a practical way of establishing the focus for the year.

The associates know when they come to the Center that the focus will be on religious experience rather than religious concepts. The most practical way of beginning to talk about religious experience is to talk about our own.

Arrangement of the Meeting

Two sessions are usually held each day. Each of these sessions consists of a brief exposition of the topic and an introduction to a biblical passage that can serve as an appropriate starting-point for prayer. Then a period of 45 minutes to an hour is devoted to individual prayer. This is followed by a meeting at which each participant has an opportunity to describe what happened when he or she tried to be receptive to God. The usual group, including the staff, numbers 9-13 participants. One to two hours are generally given to this part of the session.

At a typical meeting, the first session takes up the experience of God in the early years of a person's life, generally up to the ages of five or six. The second centers on the time from middle childhood to the making of a critical life-choice, marriage for instance, or a decision to enter a seminary or a religious congregation. The third session, which opens the second day, considers the person's experience from the making of a life-choice to close to the present time. The fourth concentrates on the person's present experience, particularly his or her decision to apply to the Center and his or her hopes for the year at the Center.

Biblical passages often proposed as starting-points for individual prayer are Psalm 139 ("Lord, you have examined me and you know me"), the first verses of Isaiah 43 ("Have no fear; for I have redeemed you; I call you by name; you are mine."), Hosea 11 ("When Israel was a youth, I loved him"), and Mark 8:29 ("And you," he asked, "who do you say I am?"). All these texts invite the participant to advert to the part God has played in his or her life and encourage the participant to respond.

A Typical Session

After the introductory session, most sessions start with the suggestion that each member of the group pray for 45 minutes or so, beginning by asking God to remind him or her of a time when God showed Godself to the person. It is also suggested that when they recall such an incident, they take time to contemplate the memory, let their feelings react to it, and perhaps speak to God about it.

We spend the time for prayer either at the house or on the beach. After returning to the living room we are invited by one of the staff to describe, to whatever extent we choose, what happened to us when we tried to be receptive to God. "No need to say everything that happened," we are told. "Anything you want to say will help." All speak who choose to, staff as well as associates.

Someone might say something like this:

The sea was glorious, with the sunlight dancing on the waves and the breakers foaming toward the shore.

As I walked along the beach I felt that I wanted to be open to anything God might show me. For a while I just looked at the sea and let myself feel calm and receptive. I was not aware of any particular memory for some time. Then all at once I remembered an incident that occurred when I must have been no more than three years old.

I was alone in my room at night. I awoke to see lightning flashing across the window and hear thunder rumbling nearby. Suddenly, I heard an ear-splitting crack of thunder and saw the whole room flare up around me. I was terrified. I must have yelled, because a minute later the door opened and my mother was holding me. I heard her saying, "I'm here; I'm here. I was only in the kitchen. I looked in and saw you sleeping." Then she said, "And God was close too and He thought of you. He

wouldn't leave you alone any more than we would."
I listened to her, rapt.

For years after that, whenever violence threatened me, I would think: "He is close and He is thinking of me." Sometimes I could almost feel Him there. And once I knew—I was so sure He was there shielding me that every vestige of fear left me, though at that moment I really was in danger. I remembered all that piece by piece after I asked God to show me when in my childhood He began to form my inner life. What the memory said to me is that with all that has been uncertain, even violent in my life, God had found a way to let me know that he would never be too far away to hear me. Even before I have called for help, He has sometimes shown me He was aware that I needed it. So I'm surprised at what I saw today when I asked Him to show me what He has been like for me. I had forgotten the storm. But there is something obvious about it too. In uncertainty and violence especially, He is the one who cares even before I call upon Him.

This account would be a helpful contribution to the dynamic that develops during the Seabrook meeting. Why so? It tells the speaker's colleagues, first of all, that he trusts them enough to describe for them an event that came to his mind while he was praying, and discloses to them something about God and himself that has been important in the development of his life. What he has told them he would not say to casual acquaintances. The account also benefits the speaker. In offering it to his colleagues, he entrusts them with a fact of his inner life that is important, even precious, to him. The telling of it and their acceptance bring him affectively closer to them, and further the growth of his trust in them.

Receptivity to One Another's Experience

How does the group receive what is said? They are asked to listen receptively, without debating and without making judgments on what is said. This is no time to engage in discussion of what constitutes a valid religious experience, for example. It is a time rather for encouragement and empathy, so that the person and the person's perception of his or her experience of God can be heard and attended to. The success of the ministry of both speaker and listeners will depend upon the willingness of men and women to reveal to them experiences of God and their deeper reactions to life. It is, then, peculiarly appropriate to their ministry that some of the first confidences they entrust to one another should pertain to their perception of God's communication in their own lives. It is also appropriate to the experience of the year they are beginning that they should encounter together the sense of risk and the fear of being subjected to behind-the-hand ridicule that often besets directees as they disclose the ways they believe they have experienced God. Besides undergoing this risk, they also become better acquainted with the satisfaction that permeates us when, after recounting an intimate experience, we realize that our hearers have not been repelled or confused by it. Occurrences like these encourage spontaneity.

Staff Members Also Participate

So far we have spoken principally of the associates' part in the meeting. But, although the associates, newly arrived at the center, occupy the central place at the meeting, they are not the only persons present who try to be receptive to God in prayer. Nor are they the only persons who reveal what happens to them when they pray. The supervisory staff, usually numbering three or four, also take part. There is little novelty to the procedure for them. In 1993 one staff member took part in his 22nd introductory meeting and another her 16th. What does their participation mean to them?

They find that something new often happens to them as they pray. When they leave themselves open to the Lord, they are as likely to be surprised by the outcome as the associates are. "Every year something different happens," they once said to one another.

Nor does their experience of previous meetings enable them to predict what will happen to the other participants. Each participant is different; each goes before God in his or her own way; and God will approach each person differently. The interaction in the particular group is also unique.

Although the staff are responsible for opening each session, and have the task of preventing the session from becoming mired or lost in tangential considerations, they also try to be as receptive to God as are the associates. This receptivity helps set the tone for their relationships with the associates during the coming year. The staff will have administrative, supervisory, and evaluative responsibilities. But at Seabrook staff and associates take the first step in what the staff hope will be the development of a basic peership. All, not only the associates, try to be receptive to God, and all try to express something of what happens when they pray. They will take another step in this development when both staff and associates begin to work as spiritual directors during the year, with one group no more spiritual directors than the other, and no more responsible for their work than the other. They will take another when both supervisory staff and associates begin to participate in the Group Life process. That we will describe later in this chapter.

Opportunity and Difficulties

The invitation to address God and be receptive to God, the opportunity for extended prayer and reflection, and the complementary opportunity to communicate their experience to willing and responsive listeners, help the participants to make explicit their faith in God's action in their lives. Such opportunities do not present themselves often to most people. Listening to another person's experience, however, is not always easy. A participant might find himself or herself too restless to listen quietly and attentively to another person's experience of God, for instance. Or he or she might be skeptical of the reality of a particular experience. Or an associate might, after another associate's striking and convincing description of an experience of God, seem to miss the point.

The last situation, which is common enough, is also important enough to warrant an example. Louis, an associate, closes his account by saying:

> I wasn't going to tell you this, but I will. There was a memory of hiking in New Hampshire, standing on a broad ledge and looking out over miles of farmland spread out below me. It was a Sunday morning last spring. I don't know how long I stood there, but God seemed closer than ever before, so close I felt God was touching me.

Jerry, another associate, comments:

> I've been up there. Some of those mountains are spectacular. Did you get to Mount Washington?

Readers who have heard people describe an experience of God in a group will recognize how readily one of the group can miss the point, as Jerry did. It can happen for many reasons; eagerness to describe an experience of one's own is among the more usual. A reason that seems to obtain more often than we usually realize, however, is a desire, whether conscious or subconscious, to turn the conversation away from the experience of God.

Despite difficulties, the level of trust is quite high during these September faith-sharing days. An atmosphere of good fellowship is usually achieved. When they arrive at the Center the associates are caring, gentle people who are able to listen to others without changing the subject. They can hear others' experience with empathy and they know how to ask questions that will encourage them to talk about themselves. These attitudes and skills give them the capacity to form a friendly, accepting group on short acquaintance.

This friendliness is not deep trust, however. Rarely if ever does a group of staff and associates reach that level at this meeting. Some participants remain guarded during these three days. They are guarded, but not reclusive. Despite their inner reserve, they often contribute to general conversation more than their share of jokes, anecdotes, and even dramatically candid accounts of embarrassing incidents in their lives. As the year goes on, they often come to have more confidence in the group, and become less watchful.

Associates often take advantage of this gathering to tell the group about events and circumstances in their lives they want to be sure the others know about. Someone may describe a difficult experience—the illness or death of a parent, for example—that took place during the summer and caused unsettlement that was not present at the admission interview. The Clinical Pastoral Education experience, which many associates complete only a few weeks before arriving at the Center, may have brought to vivid awareness disturbing facts about themselves which they have not yet assimilated.

New experiences can refocus or reshape an associate's perceptions. The September faith-sharing provides an opportune time to talk about what has happened with the other associates and staff. Untoward occurrences can also take place during the meeting itself. In two successive years recently, a near relative of one of the associates died while we were at Seabrook. There have been occasions, too, when an associate, who was accepted because of an expressed desire to do spiritual direction, announced a primary interest in personal renewal rather than in ministry.

Growing Awareness

The first meeting is on the whole a happy and productive occasion. It is also a time when some of the implications of their commitment to the program are borne in on the associates for the first time. With the gray-blue expanse of the late-summer sea stretching out on the other side of the picture window and the voice of someone they met only a few days before speaking of God in his or her life, the reality of the program takes on new bulk and vividness.

They will be together for eight months. They will affect the lives of people they do not yet know. The reputation of the Center for capable spiritual direction will depend significantly on them. They will have their ministry supervised by one of the staff members sitting nearby. The other men and women will know something of the successes and failures that will occur in the year's work.

An associate might think:

> How did I get into this? They're all so articulate about their experience, and I feel so inept when I contribute. And they've had so much experience! The fellow on my left has been a pastor and an advisor to a bishop.

The man on her left might be musing:

> The woman with the sunburned nose has told us three times that she graduated from Yale Divinity, and we're still in the first week. What's it going to be like dealing with her all year?

Another associate might be saying to herself:

> They warned me it would be hard, that some of the others have had a lot more experience of direction than I've had. But most of these people seem to have been directing for eight or nine years, and one of them has been doing it for fifteen.

Recognizing the Need for Support

During the last session of the meeting we suggest that the associates ask God to help them recognize and clarify their strongest hopes for the coming year. When they come to speak about these hopes, many associates say that, in addition to developing their abilities as spiritual directors, they hope for further personal growth. They also often say that they expect that the group will help them with this. "I think this group can help me" and "I hope this group can help me" are repeatedly expressed during this session. The statements occur in various contexts:

I hope that by the second semester I'll be less reserved and more outgoing. I think this group can help me with that.

I'll be able to build on what I learned about myself in C.P.E. now that I'm in this group. It's been good to tell you about the C.P.E. experience. Several of you have already told me how you feel about what I said.

Except for short visits, this is my first time back in the country in eight years. Everything has changed. And I'm acutely aware every time I go to a supermarket of how different life here is from the life I was immersed in during those eight years. I'll be trying to get used to all that change during the next few months. Thank God I'll have a supportive group to help me. Living alone at mission stations, you talk to yourself a lot. You get tired of that. Just being able to talk with you here has been a great treat.

Each of these men and women looks to the others for some kind of help. They find themselves, perhaps for the first time in years, with the time and opportunity to enjoy companionship with a group of people who share some of their deeper interests. They also are engaged with them in a common enterprise that promises to bring them closer together. It is, too, an enterprise they view with some uncertainty. As they say they need support, they are at least dimly aware that the need is mutual. Implicitly the note is sounded: "You're going to need my support, too."

The associates choose their own living arrangements. Except for those who have been living in the area, they arrange for accommodations in religious communities, rectories, or apartments in Cambridge or nearby cities or towns. We have often been asked whether we have thought of engaging a building where the associates could live together. This has been a usual practice with continuing education and other renewal programs established in the last two decades.

We have resisted these suggestions for long-term economic reasons. We have wanted to keep overhead low. But we have also been unwilling to undertake any project that would distract us or the associates from the primary purpose of the program. We have believed that the Center would serve that primary purpose more effectively if it limited its responsibility for the communal and social life of the associates. So we have concentrated on meeting their communal needs as a working and reflecting group, and left the choice and management of their living situations to them. The associates' experience has confirmed the soundness of this decision. They have never cited the fact they have not lived together as a factor that has detracted from the effectiveness of the program.

Communicating on the Level of Faith

We have described the topics suggested to the group and the way we propose that they approach them. We have also described what may be said and thought when the participants speak of what happened when they tried to pray. Let us now discuss further what we hope to accomplish by proposing that they recall their experience of God and do so only after asking God to remind them of ways in which God has been revealed in their lives.

"Don't try to figure out where God has been in your life," the group is told. "Ask God to let you know where God has been, and see what happens." The words are carefully chosen. What do we have in mind?

The proposal is not intended to encourage a desire for visions or auditions. It does suggest to the participants, however, that they may be able to remember instances of God revealing Godself in their lives. It also directs their attention away from themselves and from any inclination to analyze their lives. It suggests that they concentrate instead on God's interest in them and God's desire to communicate with them. It invites the person to be receptive to whatever use God might choose to make of his or her memory and ability to contemplate past experience. God may want to make no use of them at this time, or the person may be too distracted to listen. The person will nonetheless have expressed his or her desire to receive from God, and the desire, once activated and expressed, can prove productive in another session or later in the year.

The major purpose of this proposal is, then, to provide an opportunity for staff members and associates to communicate with one another on the level of their faith. "The level of their faith" requires some explanation. Many people who believe in God do not think of God as someone who wants to communicate with them.

They may think of God as a force or a power with no more ability to communicate than a lightning-bolt. Others may think God communicates with the human race in general—through the beauty, fruitfulness, and nobility of the natural world, for instance, and, if they are Christians, through the Old and New Testaments. They may never seriously ask themselves, however: Does God want to communicate with me? And does that happen?

We phrase these as questions that pertain to objective belief about God. They do. But other, more subjective questions are also of paramount importance: Do I want God to communicate with me? And will I allow God to do so? For God can communicate, but by rationalizing or trivializing that communication, I may deny it an opportunity to affect me. Without letting myself attend to what is being said, for example, I can at once begin to ask myself: How do I know this is from God? Or I can dismiss it because at first glance it does not match my expectation of what God would want to communicate to me.

These questions, vital as they are for every human being, have particular importance for the spiritual director. Central to his or her capacity to minister is the question: Is my practical belief in God's desire to communicate with us strong and active enough to let me listen attentively as people tell me what seems to be happening between God and themselves?

Unless directors can answer this question affirmatively and with some assurance, they will find ways to avoid giving their attention to God's communication. The fact that the evasion is often subconscious does not make it less evasive, or less bewildering for the directee who wants to discuss an experience that lies close to the heart of his or her spiritual life.

We will return in the next chapter to the directee's experience of God. Now, however, we want to explore further the hope we have that the first meeting at Seabrook will help associates develop a receptive attitude toward the God who wants to communicate with their directees.

The associates have all been practicing Christians, most of them for many years. The purpose of the meeting is not to invite them to faith. They are already people of faith, and they have worked with other people on the level of faith. The purpose, however, has to do with faith. Let us look at that purpose more closely.

We have said that for many people of faith God communicates with the human race, but not with individuals, especially themselves. The penetrating impression that the sight of a snow-crowned mountain conveys of the splendor of God can never be intended specifically for them. None of the minuscule miracles that they recognize in their lives ever take place because God cares individually for them. Even when for a moment they glimpse God acting on their behalf they let the awareness merge with assorted other insights that occur to them that day and lose sight of its special importance for them.

This lack of awareness can happen to people in general. It can also happen to spiritual directors, and the dimness of vision can extend far beyond particular incidents. Years of a director's ministry can be spent in a miasma that effectively blocks from the person's consciousness the activity of God on his or her behalf. The person knows that God loves him or her and may be able to discuss this knowledge at considerable length. But he or she does not react with vibrant consciousness to the enlivening, invigorating effects of the activity of God on his or her spirit. People in this situation can be competent, helpful ministers, but because they do not have a lively sense of their own experience of God, they are less likely to recognize it in other people and to respond to it with reverence and affection when they do recognize it.

The first meeting at Seabrook can begin to counteract this lethargy and dimness of vision where it is present, to whatever extent it is present. The most effective way of learning how to help other people to become aware of and respond to their experience of God is to become aware of and respond to one's own experience of God.

Recalling and describing, we hope, will begin a process of remembering and enlivening that will continue in the associates' prayer, in the spiritual direction they receive during the year, in the spiritual direction they give, and in the other "faith sharing" meetings that take place at Seabrook in the winter and spring.

The Workshop on God Acting*

In our description of the first Seabrook meeting, we spoke of the ease with which a person's account of a religious experience can be overlooked or deflected. In 1980 the staff, recognizing that this happened often in the spiritual direction given by associates during the first semester, decided that we were giving the associates too little opportunity to come to

---

* For years we used the term "religious experience" in describing this workshop. We also used it often in other contexts. Gradually over the last five years we reduced our emphasis on the term and now seldom use it at all. Instead, we use the term "God acting."
Our reason: The experience designated by the term remains crucial in spiritual direction, but it is the experience not the concept of the experience, that is so important. We realized finally that in our culture, which is unused to contemplating experience, but very accustomed to generalizing and analyzing, a term like "religious experience," which sounds intellectual, invites people to treat it as a concept, rather than look at the eyeballs turn up into the head when the term is used," one staff member said. Since we wanted the eyeballs to be fully employed with what God was doing rather than with what the director's head was doing, we have let the term fall into disuse.

grips with their reactions to this experience when they encountered it. They had heard lectures on religious experience; they had discussed directors' resistance to religious experience; their own perceptions of religious experience and reactions to it had often been discussed in individual supervision. However, there had been little or no opportunity for them as a group to become aware of what they perceived and what feelings they experienced when a directee said: "The Lord said to me . . ." or "It was as if the Lord was there with me."

To remedy this difficulty, we decided to add to the associates' program a workshop on religious experience to begin a few days after the first faith-sharing. During this workshop the associates would be encouraged to discuss their perceptions of some of the experiences they had heard during the faith-sharing meeting and the feelings with which they had reacted to those perceptions.

This workshop, two or three days long, also takes place at Seabrook. The first time we held it we found that the difficulty we hoped to resolve soon made its appearance. It has been appearing at these workshops ever since.

Eddie, an associate, says, for example: When you talked about your childhood, Frank, you described a lot of suffering. A lot of sickness, for example. What a harrowing time that must have been for you!

Frank: Yes, it was. Good thing there was more to it than the suffering. I think I said something about God.

Eddie: Oh, did you? Let's see . . . You said that you felt confidence in him.

Frank: Yes. I said that. But I think I said more than that, too.

Louise: You said, Frank, that God showed you that he was bearing the pain with you. At least that's what I remember . . .

Eddie: Oh. I didn't remember that.

This conversation illustrates interaction that is characteristic of the workshop. Eddie remembers Frank's suffering and reminds him of it. Talk about suffering—sickness, failure, disappointment—is familiar ground to most directors and they enter on it with confidence. Frank agrees that he spoke of his childhood illnesses, and then reminds Eddie that he also spoke of something else that Eddie has not mentioned.

A third person—Louise—now enters the conversation. She remembers that Frank had said God had been bearing his pain with him. Let us note two facts about Eddie's comments. He momentarily forgets that Frank spoke about God. Then, when he begins to remember, he recalls Frank's statement about God's relationship with him in general, relatively bland terms. He speaks of "confidence in God," a term familiar to anyone accustomed to the language of Christian spirituality, but a term that reflects little of the experience Frank tried to convey. When Eddie is reminded that Frank spoke of God bearing Frank's pain with him, he realizes that he does not remember that poignant part of Frank's account.

Overlooking, forgetting and generalizing are three of the ways a director loses contact with a directee's experience when, consciously or subconsciously, he or she does not want to give attention to it. Overlooking and forgetting put it out of the director's mind; generalizing substitutes contact with an idea for contact with the experience.

Recognizing the difficulty is of capital importance. Nothing can be done to remedy it unless it is recognized. It is no mere detail that Eddie has forgotten. Frank's statement that God had shown him God was bearing his pain with him is the kind of assertion that spiritual directors find of profound interest.

Of equal importance, however, is the question: What caused Eddie to forget a statement that objectively is so replete with interest for a spiritual director? Harry, one of the staff, takes the initial step in exploring this question.

Harry: Do you know what you felt when Frank reminded
us just now that God had shown him he was bearing
the pain with him?

Eddie: I felt he was talking about something that had
helped him.

Harry: No, I mean feelings. What feelings did you have?

Eddie thinks for a minute or two and then says: I was
uncomfortable.

Harry: Not at ease? Would you like to say more?

Eddie: I don't think I could right now.

Harry: It might be helpful to reflect on that and bring it
up when you start supervision.

Harry could have pursued the point. "Uncomfortable" is
far from a specific statement of Eddie's feelings. During the
workshop, however, we keep in mind that many associates
have not yet experienced supervision in depth, and some
might be alarmed by either experiencing or observing it in a
group setting this early in the program. We usually prefer to
introduce associates to it gradually, in the less public situation of individual supervision. Enough has been said to
make it clear to the associates that Eddie's forgetfulness was
probably prompted by his uneasiness. They can now begin to
ask themselves whether they too have been uneasy when a
religious experience was described, and, if they have been,
what effect their uneasiness had on them.

Associates give considerable attention in these discussions to demonstrating that they approve of one another.
Gloria may say to Elizabeth, for example:

Thank you very much for your description of your
sister's wedding. The way you spoke of the healing
it brought to your family was very graphic and very
poignant. It made me want to know you better. I
look forward to the coming months together.

This attention to one another can cause them to overlook the purpose of the workshop. After a time a staff member will comment:

We've been talking for a half-hour and no one has mentioned God yet.

This disinclination to talk about the experiences of God they have heard from one another raises a point that will be important for their ministry. Often a director becomes so absorbed in the people he or she is directing that their experiences of God are overlooked for a time. There is some advantage to this. One cannot give spiritual direction to people one does not know. But the people who come for direction come for a purpose; and that purpose has to do with God. The disinclination to talk about experiences of God reminds associates that they will need determination and self-discipline if they are to help directees talk about their religious experience and so get what they most want from spiritual direction.

The issue, of course, is not to enable associates to talk with directees about their religious experience as though it were an entity that floats free of their lives, but to enable them to talk about it appropriately, with reference to whatever else of importance is happening in their lives. Louise gives us an example of how this can be done when she says to Don:

Louise: I was captivated by your description of what your time in the Jamaican bush was like, The way you talked about the people you knew there could not have been more vivid. I could actually see those children with their shining faces and neat school uniforms heading down the hill road to the schoolhouse. Then it was very moving to hear you describe that night when you felt so lonely and Jesus seemed to be in the room with you and told you how delighted he was that you liked those people because he liked them too and how grateful he was that you could be there for them.

Don: Did I say he was grateful?

Louise: I think you did.

Don: He did seem to say that. I didn't think I had mentioned it.

A Focus for the Year

The workshop on religious experience proposes the focus for the associates' year. Their central concern in the spiritual direction they give will be the development of the directees' relationship with God. It is because they want this development that directees come to the Center. Despite this desire, however, the relationship with God can be kept at a distance in spiritual direction.

It is a basic contention at the Center that spiritual direction takes place on a new and more productive level when the directee and the director begin to speak of the directee's experience of God. The director's ability to talk about that experience is for this reason crucial to the quality of direction.

Directees are not inclined to talk about this experience unless they believe that the director wants to listen to what they have to say. They will tend to hesitate, and this tendency will be especially pronounced if in the past they tried to disclose experience to a director or other confidant who paid little attention to it. We must keep in mind that religious experience is not a concept or a group of concepts. It is not the product of thought. It is an event that has happened to a person and has tapped deep springs of feeling. People are thus far more protective of their religious experience than they are of their religious ideas.

Until a directee comes to believe that a director will take him seriously when he talks about his experience of God, he—or she—is likely to spend time in spiritual direction talking about his or her family, work, or career prospects. He may also discuss his images of God and the way he thinks about God. But the director will not hear how he experiences God.

During the workshop, associates are likely to appreciate that they have a struggle on their hands. There is something in them that does not want to listen to people's experiences of God, or may be willing to listen to some experiences of God, but not to those that are markedly different from their own experience. That appreciation will be of enormous help to them. They may, before they leave Seabrook, make some headway with the struggle. Even if they do not, they are likely to have become acquainted with the central issue of their year, and of their ministry of direction.

Spiritual Direction Develops the Faith of the Director

The September meetings at Seabrook are intended to lay a foundation for the rest of the year. The foundation is soon built upon, especially by the experience of giving direction. This experience begins late in September, the week after the faith-sharing meeting. Since directors are facilitators of the relationship with God rather than teachers or instructors, they are likely to hear people with whom they are talking begin to speak of their relationship with God early in the process of direction: who God is to them, how they came to see God like that, who they are to God, as far as they can tell, and what happens between them, as they see it. The description will be given piecemeal, over a period of weeks and months, and more will probably be disclosed as the person describes what happens when he or she tries to pray than when he or she sets out deliberately to describe the relationship. The description will often be instructive not only in what it says about the directee, but also in what it says about God. The director comes to learn about God from the directee. Associates have often learned more about God from directees than they have from supervision, courses, or any other facet of their experience at the Center.

The director learns about God from directees' experience. He or she also reacts to God as God appears in directees' experience. The reaction will be a reaction to God, but it will be colored by the director's own history with God, and by the present state of his or her own relationship with God. For example, a director who is painfully aware that he experiences God as distant and heedless may react sardonically to a directee's jubilant description of delight in God's presence. If a directee is describing God challenging her to new reaches of openness, the director who has not for some time experienced herself as open to God's action may withdraw from the directee's experience. The more concretely God's action is described, the more likely the director is to become uncertain and withdraw.

On the other hand, a director for whom prayer has become pedestrian can listen with a discoverer's delight as she learns from a directee's experience that God is more likely to respond to frank expressions of a person's spontaneous reactions than to listless descriptions of the state of his soul. And another director may ruefully acknowledge to himself after hearing a directee's description of a vibrant new awareness of God in his prayer that he himself is probably not patient enough in prayer to give God a chance to do the same thing for him.

Group Life

We have described in this chapter the structure and substance of the September meetings at Seabrook. We have also described the hope we have that these meetings will begin a development of the associates' faith that will continue as they give spiritual direction during the year. To avoid diffuseness, we will not describe the contributions we hope supervision, the courses, and the later workshops will make to that development. We will, however, explore in some detail the component of the program we call Group Life.

"Group Life" designates a gathering of the associates and supervisory staff that takes place sometimes weekly, sometimes every other week. Each session lasts an hour and a half. These gatherings were for many years facilitated by a professional facilitator who had no other responsibility at the Center. For several years now, however, the staff have facilitated the group life meetings.

An example will illustrate the immediate purpose of these gatherings. Harriet, an associate, says:

I'd like to tell you about my Uncle Ben. He's been on my mind a great deal during the last week. He has cancer and my Aunt Alice is having a lot of trouble taking care of him. I hadn't been thinking much about Ben until the day a directee, deeply upset, told me her father was dying of cancer. For five minutes while she talked about it I did not hear a word she said. Since that time I've thought about Ben and Alice a great deal.

The opportunity to talk about events in one's life that have caused strong emotional reaction is important for the person who speaks. It is also important for the life of the group. Emotional currents that, unexpressed, would nevertheless affect the person's relationships are brought to the surface and described. The group can then come to terms with the feelings and not be nonplused by currents they are dimly aware of, but cannot identify.

Even more important, however, for the long-term development of directors is the opportunity Group Life provides for learning to express thoughts, feelings and affective attitudes that may rarely have been expressed to anyone. It has been a cardinal belief at the Center that spiritual directors, engaged as they are with strong forces that work in people's lives, need for their own sake and that of the people they work with to be able to talk to one another about their reactions to their lives and their ministry.

We give particular attention to affective reactions that can occur in direction. Any director who engages sensitively with other people's experience has affective reactions to that engagement. These reactions, if they are kept confined within oneself, tend to gather force and accumulate. As a result, directors can become impatient with some directees, unobservant of others, arbitrarily skeptical of the experience of some of the people they talk to, or worn out by the sheer effort of responding to the intensity of the emotions with which they engage. This is not hard to understand. Listening to and responding to people's experience of God, they are engaged with the deepest forces in a person's life and they react to them. Open, frank communication of their reactions to responsible peers engaged in the same ministry can help them continue to encounter these forces with assurance and equanimity.

Many of us, however, have had little practice expressing our deeper feelings. If we are to express them to peers who are not intimate friends, we have to learn to do so. One of the primary purposes of the Group Life meetings is to give both staff and associates opportunities to practice expressing our feelings to our colleagues and to allow them to express their feelings to us. No program gives a person the ability to communicate at deeper levels. He or she learns to do so by making repeated attempts, some of them labored, some of them abortive. Other members of the group usually take an encouraging, receptive attitude toward those who speak. They may be loath to speak themselves, however, and when this reluctance besets most of those in the group, long, tedious silences can result.

Once this ability to communicate with colleagues begins to be acquired through repeated efforts, a director has a basis for future communication with other directors that is different from the intellectual, often subtly competitive attitude many professional people adopt toward their colleagues. This competitive, defensive attitude would make peer supervision difficult or impossible. Directors who do not discuss their ministry candidly with other directors may think:

> "It's too much trouble."

> or

> "I already know the answer. I have to be more relaxed, and who can do that but myself?"

Rarely will they think:

> "I'm not able to tell my peers what affects me most deeply in my ministry."

A pivotal fact that they overlook is that they are neglecting a resource that can be of great and continuing help in their ministerial life. A second fact, one of which they may be unaware, is that they are neglecting this resource because they have never learned to make use of it.

Many of the Center's former associates have a reputation among other directors for their determination to avail themselves of group supervision. This determination is prevalent among them, we believe, because they have learned through repeated practice how to communicate with their peers about issues to which they are personally sensitive. Though not everyone makes extensive use of it, Group Life has an important part to play in developing the ability to make use of this resource.

Peership Between Staff and Associates in Group Life

At Group Life meetings both staff and associates are invited to say what they think and feel. When they take part in these meetings, staff members do not cease to be supervisors, administrators, and teachers. No one in the room forgets that they have these responsibilities, least of all themselves. They are not there, however, to supervise, administer, or teach, but, like everyone else, to listen and say what they feel and think. Staff and associates thus find in Group Life a particularly valuable opportunity to develop the fundamental peership the staff hope will grow among them. It does not do so without vicissitudes and difficulty. But the opportunity is there.

When the year ends, peership remains an ideal that has been only partly realized. The teachers and supervisors, though they often have learned much from their interaction with those they have taught and supervised, have remained the teachers and supervisors. And the associates have continued to experience the medley of attitudes that those who participate in any supervisory program have toward those in. charge of the program. The "we-they" distinction does not disappear and the feelings that stem from it are not effaced.

The hope that we can come closer to realizing the ideal does not fade either. There has been a steady striving to be more candid with one another. Staff members have learned in the last few years, for example, to address more directly signs of malaise they see appearing in the group. Decisions that will affect all of us and are not the responsibility of the staff alone have more frequently been handed over to the whole group.

Group Life and the Development of Faith

Group life at first glance appears to be a simple and inviting procedure. In practice, it is a test of maturity. The ability and willingness to participate fully in it come hard to an underdeveloped person. By the same token, it is an invitation to let the underdeveloped aspects of ourselves come closer to full maturity.

Group life is also an invitation to a more mature faith. A developing faith does not stand in isolation from the person's practical attitude toward human relationships. It empowers the person's trust in these relationships. It derives fiber and breadth from the person's experience of them.

Before I can responsibly give trust, the other person has to show himself or herself trustworthy. But when the other person has done this, I do not automatically bestow my trust. I have to decide to bestow it. Group life, as the year goes on and we come to know one another better, presents us repeatedly with opportunities to bestow trust by letting more of ourselves enter our communication with one another. As we recognize and surmount the barriers to open communication that exist within ourselves, we become better able to recognize and clamber over those barriers when they impede our communication with God. As we come to surmount them, we find ourselves more receptive to God's communication with us. For God, too, can show Godself trustworthy and yet may not be responded to. When we do respond, one result is likely to be still more responsiveness to one another.

Continuing Attention to the Psychological Dimension

One element of the C.R.D. program, featuring all-day sessions scheduled occasionally throughout the academic year, focuses the associates' attention upon the psychological and psychiatric aspects to be found in the spiritual lives of their directees. Taught by priest-psychiatrist James J. Gill, SJ, this series of conversations examines the normal stages of psychosexual and social development, basic human needs, unconscious defense mechanisms, the difference between healthy and pathological fantasies and feelings, and ways of dealing with the transference and countertransference phenomena likely to present themselves in the course of spiritual direction.

At the start of the year, Jim assists the associates to develop a collaborative attitude, so that mutual support can enable these already experienced directors to share their learning and skills for the benefit of each one's professional progress. As the year goes on, he discusses with them such issues as guilt and shame in relation to conscience, problems related to initiating and terminating direction, ways of referring directees to psychiatrists when evaluation or treatment is needed, and how to distinguish clinical depression from the spiritual experience known as "the dark night of the soul."

Jim helps the associates to develop a habit of maintaining a wise balance including the work, spiritual, social, cultural and physical aspects of their own lives. He teaches them about the relationship between stress and illness, strategies to avoid burnout, and the latest scientific findings regarding the mind/body interaction in health and disease. Throughout the year, Jim is available to the associates for consultation whenever they are faced with direction situations that show signs of pathology. He is also helpful to the staff as a consultant always ready to assist them when supervision of the associates brings up a question about the anxieties, frustrations or ambivalences that arise from time to time in any prolonged or intense helping relationship.

Chapter Six

What Spiritual Direction Is Like at the Center

"Spiritual direction" is not a self-explanatory term. In the course of Christian history, spiritual direction has had many faces. This variety has been especially evident in the last two decades. Since spiritual direction is the central occupation at the Center, a coherent understanding of the Center's ministry requires a somewhat detailed description of how we approach spiritual direction. The description will take its point of view from the experience of what actually happens when direction takes place.

This chapter will first show what spiritual direction at the Center looks like, then will describe the process of direction as the director perceives it.

What Does Spiritual Direction Look Like?

"Do you have any photographs of spiritual direction?" one of us was once asked during the preparation of an article for a newspaper. "What would you photograph?" was the reply. "You would only see two people talking." The answer could hardly have been helpful to an editor in need of illustrations, but it accentuates a point that deserves our attention as we begin to describe direction. There are no vestments, no rituals, no formalities to spiritual direction. For the sake of clarity and brevity, we will call one of the two people conversing the directee, and the other the director. But the difference between them lies in the different purposes they have in talking, not in the clothes they wear or the furnishings at their disposal. The director does not sit behind a desk, consult an array of books, or deliver homilies to a respectful listener. He or she may not even give advice. As they begin their work, they may discuss the unusually clear weather or the crowded condition of the parking lot. They look like what they are: just two people talking.

Since the primary purpose of direction is the development of the directee's relationship with God, a directee's desire to pray during or after an interview is never seen as incidental to the interview. It is the natural outcome to the two people talking, always to be hoped for, but never to be achieved by programming or stratagem. When directees pray, they do so freely, because they have decided to pray.

Do directee and director pray together? Usually they do not. Most directors at the Center believe that a routine of praying together at the beginning or end of meetings would interfere with the free, relaxed atmosphere they hope for in direction. Relatively seldom, as a result, is time reserved for prayer during direction interviews. Sometimes, however, a directee asks a director to join him or her in prayer. For example, a directee might say at the end of a meeting:

> I'm amazed that I've become so clear about this today. I'd like to thank God for that. Would you pray with me?

Clearly the initiative has been taken by the directee. The director would want to encourage that initiative, remembering that the purpose of the direction is the directee's prayer. So he or she might say something like this:

> I'd be glad to pray with you. Why don't we take a moment of quiet and you can begin when you're ready?

The director participates as one who is affirming and encouraging the other in prayer. He or she might thank God for what has happened between the directee and God as the director hears that described, but would not in any way move the focus of the prayer toward him/herself.

When a director thinks a directee might like to pray, though the directee has not raised the question explicitly, he or she might make the suggestion:

> The last week seems to have been an important time for you. You may want to spend a few minutes in our prayer room before you leave or thank God sometime during the week for all that has happened. How does that sound to you?

This again leaves the decision to pray with the directee. The directee remains in charge of when, how, and even whether he or she will speak to God.

The following remarks by Tom, a fairly typical priest director, point up another possible difficulty about praying with directees that is worth our attention:

> After several months of praying often with my directees, I discovered that I had developed a little formula for every occasion. I felt like a greeting card! When I stopped to look at what was going on, I realized that I didn't always feel like praying from my heart. I was motivated by the idea that a good spiritual director should be able to pray anytime and anywhere with his directees.

Tom went on to say that he was now trying to be more true to himself. If one of his directees wanted to pray, he suggested that they pray in silence.

> Then I tell the person that if either of us wants to pray aloud, we can go ahead and do so. That seems to work out well. A great deal of the time I am silent. I feel freer and it seems quite satisfactory to the directees.

Related to the question of prayer together is another question that Catholics sometimes ask: can one, or should one, receive the sacrament of reconciliation from the director when the director is a priest? Sometimes directees request the sacrament at the Center, but we do not consider the sacrament an ordinary part of the process of direction. Most directees do not ask that it be administered during direction interviews.

When directees do indicate an interest or a need, a priest will sometimes suggest making arrangements with another priest on the staff. This is done because the emotional response to a "confessor" can be quite different from the response to a director, and could influence the relationship with the director. Both tasks are true ministerial service. But the confessor is often perceived as a judge. He may be a merciful and compassionate person, but can remain in the eyes of the directee the one who imposes sanctions and levies fines. He can exercise the awesome power to forgive and the more frightening power not to forgive. The spiritual director does not exercise these powers. Experience seems to have shown many directors that it is easier for directees to talk freely and reveal themselves more readily when the question of confession to the director is not an issue.

How Direction Begins

The directee and the director usually try to bring the directee's hopes for direction into clear focus during their first meeting. The director will want to know what has prompted the directee to ask for direction. He or she might ask after the conversation has proceeded for some time:

So the idea of direction is not new to you. You've thought about it awhile. Then this summer you decided to do something. What got you to make the decision?

The director has more than information in mind when he asks this question. He wants to invite the directee to recall the event that brought him or her to direction and to talk about it.

No one begins direction in a vacuum. Often an external event has led the directee to begin direction. It may have been a conversation with a friend, an opportunity to change careers, or an illness. Whatever it was, the director hopes the directee will recall it, look at it again, and to some extent relive it. If it is significant, as it usually is, he is willing to join the directee in the recalling and reliving. Together they may see more of the experience than the directee alone could see. The director is particularly interested in giving the directee an opportunity to put the memory of the event into words, because this objectifying will enable the directee to contemplate the event more thoroughly and realize more keenly how it influenced him or her.

For internal events have also occurred. The external occurrence has affected the directee's thinking and has aroused feeling—reactions. These in turn have prompted the directee to take action. The more fully the directee contemplates the external event, the more poignantly he will be aware of the thoughts and feelings it awakened. As he contemplates these thoughts and experiences these feelings again, he will be better able to explore the desires that brought him to direction. This is a matter of considerable moment for him. His desire will be, except for God's action, the most helpful resource available to him in pursuing what he is looking for in direction. The more fully his mind and feelings lay hold of it, and the more tangibly he grasps its strength, the more forcefully it will influence him as he approaches the choices that lie before him in the early stages of direction.

What can the director do to help him explore these events? Let us begin with an example. A directee and a director have discussed the directee's reasons for asking for direction. Then the director says:

> Is there anything that got you to look for direction now? You've thought about it for the last year, but a month ago you made up your mind. What happened then that got you to decide?

Directee: I had my fortieth birthday.

Director: That's an event all right. Congratulations!

Directee: Thanks. Well, birthdays always make me stop and think. This time I thought a lot. "Forty" has a pretty solemn tone to it. My life's half over. There are a lot of things I've wanted to do and haven't done. One of them is to get serious about God.

The directee has mentioned an external event: he has had his fortieth birthday. He has also experienced an interior event: the birthday has affected his thoughts and, it appears, his feelings.

Director: It sounds as though the birthday made an impression.

Directee: Like a punch in the jaw. I had heard that you give spiritual guidance here, so I looked up your number and I picked up the phone. (He pauses.) But

I didn't call.

Director: You decided not to?

Directee: I thought: Wait a minute! What am I getting into here? I put down the phone and waited a couple of days.

Director: You waited.

Directee: And thought. And prayed. Then I called.

The directee has spoken of interior events: his hesitation, thought, and prayer. The director can overlook the possibility of exploring them. If he does, the directee will probably say no more about them. The director can, however, say:

Director: Remember what you thought and prayed about?

Directee: I thought—well, I thought: This is a very big step. This means letting someone else hear thoughts I've never spoken aloud.

Director: Letting someone hear what you've never heard yourself. Good reason to hesitate.

Directee: I wrestled with that.

Director: You wrestled with it. Quite a match?

Directee: I didn't want to come. I thought: The director won't understand what I'm talking about, and if that happens, I probably won't know what I'm talking about either. I get tongue-tied sometimes. Especially when I'm talking about things I'm not used to talking about, things that are important to me. I kept thinking: Who needs it? Then I said to myself: You need it. After awhile I remembered something Frank told me about you people. He's the friend who told me about this place. He said his director never rushed him. He said I could always take my time. Remembering that was reassuring.

Director: Gosh, you went through a lot. It was important that you'd be able to take your own time.

Directee: It was. I want to find the God who calls me, and not get bogged down in someone else's thoughts.

Director: To find the God who calls you.

Directee: Yes. To find him. That's why I wanted to come.

Director: You seem emphatic about that. He calls you, and you want to find him.

Directee: I don't want anything to get in the way of that.

Director: Would this be a good time to say more about him calling and your desire to find him?

Having experienced the director's willingness and ability to understand his hesitation, fear, and new assurance, the directee has now risked speaking of something still more intimate. He has begun to talk about God and about the desire to find God that underlies his request for direction. The director has shown him that he understands he has begun to talk about God. The director has indicated, too, that he is willing to talk further about God and the directee's desire for God. He has also left it to the directee to decide whether to pursue the matter further at this time. The directee may choose not to accept the director's invitation, but the director's attentiveness to the inner events he has already mentioned have given him reason to expect that he will also be attentive when the directee speaks further about God and himself.

Conversations like the one we have just studied, when we present them as role-plays at workshops on spiritual direction, often elicit objections from observers. "The directee is doing all the work," they say. "The director isn't doing anything." The director may rejoin that he feels tired after the conversation, and believes that he has worked. It is true, however, that it is the directee, not the director, who has tried to recall the events that have provided the substance of the conversation, and sought out the words to express them. It is he who will make the decision to speak further about God's relationship with him. This is no accident. It is important that it be so. No matter how telling a part the director takes in the process of direction, *it is the directee who makes all the decisions.* If he does not make them, direction comes to a standstill. The efforts the directee expends in the early interviews help him develop a habit of work and a momentum that will serve him well later, both in direction itself and in prayer. Among the most useful favors a director can do a directee in the early interviews is to refuse to do the directee's work for him, and to let the directee expend the effort that will enable him to develop this momentum.

Listening to the Directee's Experience

The principal issue in the conversations between the directee and the director is the directee's experience. This is the case at the beginning of direction, as we have indicated in the preceding pages. It remains true through the course of direction. The directee's experience changes, but it remains the principal issue.

Once we have grasped the centrality of the directee's experience, we can readily understand that the director's fundamental task is listening. It is first of all through listening that he or she can help the directee to bring the experience that has persuaded him to undertake direction out of the private world of his thoughts, feelings, and desires into the conversation that takes place between them. 'Directees acknowledge the fundamental nature of this task when they say, as they often do about directors who are not helpful: "He doesn't listen." Unless the director listens, spiritual direction cannot proceed.

"It seemed an easy job, sitting there listening," directors say as they describe their first reactions to the prospect of adopting direction as a ministry. It does appear easy, and listening is a simple service. Directees often let us know, however, that they have found it hard to come by people, even directors, who are able to provide it.

The listening that takes place when the director is performing this fundamental task is far more, however, than the act of attending to words. It is also participation in the directee's attempt to describe his experience so that directee and director can contemplate it together.

We will use another example to show what this participation involves. Phil, who comes to Bob for direction, is describing a recent experience that he believes has something to do with his relationship with God.

Phil: I was hiking alone through a forest. It was toward the end of the summer, and the foliage was luxuriant. The highway and the noise of the traffic were far behind me. There was no wind. The woods seemed absolutely silent. It occurred to me that the forest seemed as limitless as the sea. It encompassed me. Branches arched over my head and roots lay under my feet. I felt immersed in it, as you might be immersed in the ocean. I noticed something else too. Little by little I became aware of the profusion of living things around me. A cluster of large ferns sprouted beside the trail; a branch with maple-like leaves brushed against me; a spray of tiny blue flowers nestled against a boulder. I noticed these. But what I became most aware of was the leaves, thousands of them around me and above me, all slightly stirring. Suddenly I was astonished at the abundance of all that life. (He pauses.) I thought: I'm not alone. (He pauses again.)

Bob: All that abundance and you thought: I'm not alone.

Phil: Yes. I'm not alone. That's what I thought. I stopped and stood for a long time. I wasn't aware of the time, but I realized later it was a long time.

Bob: You stood there.

Phil: Yes. Listening.

Bob: Listening?

Phil: Listening to the silence. That's a strange thing to say, isn't it?

Bob: Say more.

Phil: It was as though the silence was full of life and was telling me something. As though something was being said that I couldn't make out. As though someone responsible for all that life was speaking.

Bob: As though someone was speaking?

Phil: Yes, and telling me . . . well, after awhile it sounded as though there was care for me. As though I were a swimmer immersed in care for me.

Why doesn't Bob ask questions like "Do you think you could have been imagining this?" or "Have you ever had an experience like this before?" What do you think Bob is trying to do?

When we ask these questions of workshop participants, someone usually answers: "You're using non-directive counseling techniques." To this, when we have our wits about us, we reply: "That's what it sounds like. But what is Bob trying to do?"

If Bob asked: "Do you think you were imagining this?" or "Have you ever had an experience like this before?" he would be distracting Phil from the attention he is giving to the experience. The distraction might be only momentary, but it would still be a distraction. All the director's comments and questions are aimed at helping Phil keep his attention on the event he is describing. Phil is absorbed in the experience, and Bob is absorbed in it with him.

Bob may also be curious. He may want to know whether Phil has had experiences like this on other occasions, but he does not let his curiosity interfere with the absorption. It might be helpful to Phil to try to remember similar experiences in another interview, or later in the same conversation, but the attention he is giving to the experience now is too important to be interrupted.

Most of us are not accustomed to standing and looking. We are attracted by the majesty of mountain views, the swirling power of blizzards, the gradually deepening color of high clouds as sunrise approaches, and by God. But we tend to glance at them and quickly turn our attention to other objects or other concerns. We give a moment's attention, but we turn away before we can become absorbed enough in what we see to be more than superficially affected by it.

Bob does what he does because he wants to give Phil a chance to be more than superficially affected by his experience in the forest. Whether Phil will return to the memory of the experience and let it form a basis for reflection and prayer, he has to decide for himself. Bob may ask him whether he would like to do this. But Bob has already done something that is likely to be more conducive to further reflection and prayer than a suggestion will be. By his interest in and engagement with Phil's experience, he has helped him pay attention to it long enough to become absorbed in it again and be further influenced by it. To let the memory become a basis for prayer will be easier because this conversation took place. In fact, Phil may have begun to pray during the conversation itself.

Helping the Directee to Contemplate God

In his conversation with Phil, Bob made no attempt to focus Phil's attention on God. Though he reflected it back, he did not add his own emphasis to Phil's remark "I'm not alone," for example. Instead, he continued to let Phil describe what had happened in his own way, at his own pace, and to decide for himself what course the account would take. He also wanted Phil to choose his own emphasis and to recognize for himself what he was emphasizing. When, therefore, Phil remarked that it was as though someone responsible for the life around him was speaking, Bob did not ask him to be more specific. He said simply: "As though someone was speaking?" Phil then mentioned that he was aware, there in the forest, that there was care for him.

We interrupted the conversation at a point at which Phil might pause to reflect. Realizing that someone cares for me has a different effect on me than recognizing that someone is talking to me. Phil has reason to pause.

What should Bob do now? We have come to a point in the conversation that proves to be a crux for directors. Both Bob and Phil are contemplating Phil's experience. Bob may think he knows that someone was speaking to Phil, and that the someone cared for him. Bob may not be sure, however, that Phil knows this, or, if he does know it, that he is willing to admit it. Many directors would say that Bob should now "lead" Phil to the knowledge Bob already has. Bob, however, chooses not to lead Phil, but to let him come to his own knowledge or his own admission. Can Bob help? He can help by encouraging Phil to keep looking at his experience and what it was making known to him.

It is, after all, Phil's experience, not Bob's. Bob will do well to let Phil keep looking until he finds out for himself what the silence is telling him. For there is more than an intellectual answer at issue. If God is speaking through the silence, the issue has to do with his relationship with Phil, and that will have to be lived out, not merely thought out.

How a relationship is to be lived out has to be determined by the persons who are relating to one another. People's experience of prayer, however, makes it clear that a relationship with God involves coming to know God rather than simply to know about God. When Bob encourages Phil to pay further attention to the silence, he expects that in God's time and in Phil's, this will mean that Phil will pay attention to God as God wants to disclose Godself. Bob hopes, too, that this attention will have no practical agenda, but will be engaged in for its own sake: to come to know God as God is intent on revealing Godself in the relationship with Phil.

Helping Directees Pay Attention to Their Feeling-Reactions

A director will not, therefore, view a directee's experience of God as he would a sighting of Halley's comet or a first glimpse of the Grand Canyon. What the directee perceives is important. Also important, however, is the directee's feeling-reaction to what he or she has perceived.

In the conversation between Bob and Phil, after he and Phil had explored Phil's perception of his experience, Bob would ask:

How did it make you feel?

Phil might reply: Feel? What do you mean?

Bob: Were .your feelings affected? Did your body tense? Did your skin get prickly?

Phil laughs: No, no. I felt good.

Bob: Good?

Phil: I felt very good.

Bob: Do you have another word for it?

Phil: Well, wait a minute. (Long pause.) I felt warm. It was a kind of softening feeling, I suppose. I had forgotten that.

The purpose of these questions is not to undertake an extensive exploration of Phil's feelings and so depart from the contemplative thrust of the conversation. Bob is inviting Phil to pay attention to the way he participated in the experience, to Phil's side of the relationship. He begins, not with his deliberate participation, but with his involuntary, spontaneous participation, which will show itself in his feeling-reactions. Phil has now begun a new phase of his description. When I begin to describe my feelings I begin to describe myself, and the more specifically and concretely I describe my feelings, the more explicitly I reveal myself. I disclose myself, not only to the person to whom I am talking, but to myself as well. A person describing his feelings about a religious experience will often explain: "I had no idea I felt like that! It was only as I described my feelings to you that I realized what they were."

This moment of self-revelation is a delicate juncture in the conversation. The person describing his feelings may want to stop doing so now. He may disengage, for example, by resorting to general descriptives like "good," "not too bad," or "all right," which reveal little about his personal reactions. If this happens, the director has to decide whether to ask for further description of his feelings, or let the matter rest. His primary purpose at this point is not to learn more about the directee's feelings, but to offer the directee an opportunity to express himself more completely to God. If he believes that the directee now knows his feelings well enough to say concretely what he feels to God, he may not pursue the subject further. He may say simply: "You don't have to say any more about your feelings to me. How do you feel, though, about saying them as completely and concretely as you can to God?" If he is in doubt, he may ask the directee whether he thinks he knows his feelings well enough to say them to God.

The decision is significant because of the consequences it is likely to have. If the directee does not express his feelings concretely to God, he is liable to find that further attempts at prayer will prove flat and lifeless. If he does express himself concretely and immediately, he may find that God will reveal Godself further. The more frankly I disclose my feelings to God, the more God seems to want to communicate Godself to me. A director's caution, if it reinforces the directee's hesitation, can make it more difficult for the directee to get what he most wants from direction.

The first attempts to express feelings to God are a beginning. The person's deeper feelings may come only gradually into his consciousness, so it may be weeks or months before he expresses them fully. In the meantime, the attention he gives to letting the feelings of which he is aware come before God gradually furthers the directee's communication with him. The director does what he can by encouraging the directee to persist in quiet but sustained attention to this communication.

It will be important during this time that the directee not divert his effort to communicate feeling into a self-absorbed exploration of his feelings. We easily become fascinated by such explorations, and without a director's help can be drawn into them without realizing that they are distracting us from our main purpose.

The principal purpose of letting ourselves become aware of our feelings in prayer is the communication of ourselves to God. This requires, however, not only self-awareness, but trust in the other person. We do not disclose our feelings, especially our deeper feelings, to those we do not trust to receive and accept them.

Helping the Directee to Interact with God

Looking at and listening to God, indispensable as they are for spiritual growth, can still leave a person passive before God. To begin to interact with God, a person must lay hold of his experience of God. He can do this by making up his mind to trust God as he has experienced God.

We cannot, however, force ourselves to trust. Tightening jaw muscles and gritting teeth will not achieve trust. Before we trust another person in delicate matters we have to recognize him or her to be trustworthy. Yet knowing a person to be trustworthy is not the same as trusting him or her. Directees say "I trust God," and we sometimes learn they are expressing a vague belief that God is trustworthy, not a conviction based on experience that they can count on God. Before we come to trust God in a matter that is important to us, we have to take a chance on God. Many who say "I trust God" have not yet trusted God enough, for example, to express to God their most intimate feelings—their deepest fears, their fiercest resentments, their most tremulous attachments. As a result, their relationship with God is at least somewhat lacking in spontaneity, and their prayer tends to be somewhat guarded.

The astute director, knowing that trust usually develops gradually at the directee's own pace, will keep pointing to opportunities for expressing more intimate feelings, but will not be demanding.

A religious experience is of inestimable value in itself, apart from the moral, psychological, or social development that may follow from it. The fact that it has occurred is itself precious. It is worth remarking that if a director is preoccupied with the moral, psychological, or social growth of a directee, he may not give his or her religious experience the attention it deserves. If he does continue to give it attention, what can happen?

In the conversation between Bob and Phil, after they have talked about Phil's feeling-reactions to his experience—

and they would do so at greater length than we have described—Bob might ask:

> Now that you've thought and talked about the incident in the forest, does anything about it stand out prominently in your mind?

Phil: It seems to me that God was doing something for me.

Bob: Doing something for you?

Phil: Going out of his way for me. Doing something special.

Bob: That's saying a lot.

Phil: I know. I feel strange saying it. I'm not used to thinking that God would go out of his way for me.

Bob: I don't know whether you want to say more about it or be quiet and ponder it. Or change the subject.

Phil: It means a lot to me. Could I be quiet with it for a minute?

Bob: Sure, take your time.

> *Phil*, after a long pause: I can't get over the care he seemed to be showing me. All I want to do just now is be aware of it and let it sink in.

Phil and Bob end the conversation here. They resume it the next time they meet, a week later.

Phil: I didn't have much time to pray this week. Life gets hectic at this time of the year. This week was the worst yet.

Bob: Pretty wild, eh?

Phil: It sure was.

Bob: Did you have a chance to think about what we were discussing last week?

Phil: That's what was so disappointing. I had hardly any opportunity to do that.

Bob: Did you think about it at all?

Phil: Not much.

Readers with little experience of direction may be puzzled by the contrast between Phil's diffidence at this meeting and the enthusiasm he showed at the end of the last interview. Those with more experience will find the reversal familiar. Both enthusiasm and diffidence are genuine. Both are reactions to the experience in the forest and the conversation about it. Bob, by his careful attention to Phil's freedom, has provided an opportunity for both reactions to develop. He could now be daunted by Phil's hesitation and change the subject. He does not do so.

Bob: Remember what you thought when it passed through your mind?

Phil: I was glad it happened. It was a wonderful experience. But I don't know what to do with it.

Bob: Did you trust it?

Phil: Trust it? What do you mean?

Bob: Sometimes a person can doubt that he really had an experience, or wonder whether God had anything to do with it.

"Do you trust it?" With this question Bob has raised a key issue. Phil has been attracted by his experience in the forest. He has talked about it and reflected on it with enthusiasm. He may not, however, have asked himself whether he trusts it. He has been accustomed to hearing about God and reading about God. But he experiences many perceptions every day, and many of them are moving, some of them deeply so. Most of them, however, give place quickly to newer, fresher perceptions, leaving little impression on his thought and his life. Bob knows that Phil may want to grasp his memory of the experience in the forest and not let it slip away. He may be willing to build on it by letting it be a focus for his prayer and reflection and, perhaps in time, a basis for action. His question offers Phil the possibility of deliberately acknowledging the reality of his experience. This acknowledgement, if he is willing to make it, will provide Phil with a foundation on which he can build. "Do you trust it?" affords him an opportunity to establish that foundation.

People who are beginning to be aware of their experience of God are not usually consistent in their willingness to trust the experience enough to build on it. They are often satisfied to have had the experience. It does not occur to them that their habitual way of perceiving their relationship with God can now change, and that their expectations of God can change too. They vacillate for a time between the new perception and their older, habitual perceptions of God. So they may be convinced today that God has now shown Godself caring for them. Yet they may not give themselves a chance to pray again for weeks.

This vacillation can be further illustrated by another example of a situation in which it frequently occurs. A directee has had an experience of God's care. He or she is delighted by the experience. A few weeks later someone dear to the directee becomes grievously ill. The directee thinks, believes, and prays now as though the experience of God's care had never taken place. Indeed, he or she may forget that it did.

Any disappointment that cuts us to the quick can bring surging back into our consciousness childhood fears of a God who was then perceived as arbitrary or vindictive. We may say, and mean it, that God cares for us, and that God's love is unconditional. But our older, more compelling perception tells us otherwise, so we withdraw from God as we would from any arbitrary or vindictive being who has power over us. We avoid affective contact with God. We may not pray at all, except to ask perfunctorily for help; or if we do try to pray more extensively, we may recognize no feeling at all, and find ourselves so harried by distractions that we can pay no attention to God. When this happens, a director will spend a significant part of the time with us asking: "Do you remember?"

"Do You Remember?"

This will not be his only task. He will listen to the directee's experience of disappointment and will explore with him his conscious feelings. He may also ask whether the disappointment and fear remind the directee of other occasions when those feelings were aroused. If he is wise, he will avoid the extensive probing of feelings that is the proper province of psychotherapy. His major task will be that of asking the directee whether he recalls any experience that has shown God to be other than fearsome, to be instead loving, caring, and inviting the directee to freedom.

When he asks about such an experience the director is not implying that the directee should view God as loving and caring now. The directee may not be able to do this, and guilt at being unable to do it would be only another useless burden. He is intimating, however, that the directee, once he recalls an experience that shows God as other than harsh and unfeeling, might decide whether he is willing to let that experience affect him too.

A person unsettled by mishaps or torn by tragedy can find it supremely difficult to let himself be absorbed again in the memory of an experience that revealed God loving him and caring for him. Grief, chagrin, and resentment are powerful emotions that can absorb our attention like quicksand, and they are especially potent when people try to quiet their minds for prayer. "When I try to quiet down, those feelings come in on me," directees will say.

Often a person harassed by such emotions who wants to engage in prayer of more than a few minutes' duration can do so only if he addresses the emotions themselves to God. This frequently permits him to become aware of God and pay attention to him. If his awareness of God is dominated by a lurking suspicion that God is harsh and arbitrary, he will find this difficult to do. The violence of his emotions will also make it hard for him to listen to any suggestion that God might not be as harsh as the directee's perceptions make God seem. If the director is patient and discreet, however, he can usually find opportunities to invite the directee to recall an experience of God as other than harsh and arbitrary. God, in God's time, can make use of such an invitation.

At stake when a directee has experienced God as caring and trustworthy but is now oppressed by a more deeply entrenched impression of God as harsh and vengeful is the directee's freedom to allow God to be Godself with him. The older impression overwhelms the memory of any newer experience that shows God to be different.

It is easy for a director to neglect his facilitative task at a time like this, and take on the role of teacher. "You have to remember the experience you described to me a few weeks ago, and what it taught you" can come readily to his lips when the directee is intransigently expressing his discouragement. Only if he is doggedly convinced that he can best serve the directee by encouraging him to pay attention to God as God chooses to show Godself can the director provide lasting help.

It may take weeks or months of weekly meetings before the director's patience and concern take effect. During this time he will be better able to maintain his facilitative posture if he relies more on the directee's memory than on his own and keeps inviting the directee to relive his experience of God caring as the directee himself recalls it. "I seem to remember something that happened a few months ago when you were hiking in the forest," he can say. "You'll remember it better than I. Can you recall it for me?"

The Director As Facilitator

Another example will help make clearer the struggle a directee may have to undergo in choosing between older attitudes toward God and newer attitudes suggested by recent experience. It will also illustrate the facilitative attitude a director can take in assisting the directee.

Mary is a friendly, engaging woman in her middle 50s, a member of a religious congregation. She has been a school teacher for more than 30 years. She is a capable teacher and has a degree of enthusiasm for her work that younger teachers envy.

Until six months ago, she perceived God basically as a guardian of law and of the regulations that govern her religious congregation. Prayer had always been something of an ordeal for her. It often centered around what was expected of her, and she frequently asked God's help to accomplish what she was "supposed to do." Sometimes, especially when she felt oppressed, she asked God what was wanted of her, but since she always thought she knew, she never waited for a reply.

Six months ago she had an experience in prayer that made her aware that God cared for her exactly as she was, with all the quirks that embarrassed her and the pettiness she tried to hide even from herself. "But I'm as petulant and inconsistent as a six-year-old," she cried out to God. "Doesn't that matter to you?" At that moment she had a very strong sense that somehow God was letting her know that what mattered so bitterly to her did not diminish God's care and affection for her.

After that incident she became increasingly able to express her deeper feelings spontaneously to God. "When I talk to him," she said to Roger, her director, "I start sentences without knowing how I'm going to finish them. It's such a delight to be that carefree with someone who loves you." At the same time she began to find herself markedly less guarded with two of the women with whom she lived. One memorable day she overheard a student say of her, "It is such fun to hear her talk about God now!" She experienced weeks of calm and uninterrupted joy. "I never thought," she told Roger, "that I could be this happy again."

Then, six weeks ago, her younger sister was found to have terminal cancer. Several days later, her sister's youngest son, a boy of whom Mary is especially fond, was seriously injured in an automobile accident. It is still not known whether he will regain the use of his right arm.

Mary has visited her sister and her nephew every day since they entered the hospital. She has been indefatigable in her efforts to encourage them and the other members of their family. During these weeks she has prayed frequently for her sister and her nephew, but has not resumed the intimate prayer in which she was engaged before her sister's illness was diagnosed. A week ago Roger asked her: "Do you think God has any interest in what has happened to you and your family?" She answered: "I don't know. He seems to be employed full-time on the moon."

Mary realizes that she is grieving and that she must expect to experience strong and diverse emotions. She and Roger have spoken of this, and she has gradually become able to express to him much of what she feels. But she remains troubled because God is so distant and seems to show so little concern for her. When Roger asks her whether she could tell God how she feels, she replies that there seems little point to doing that. After a long pause she replies bitterly: "You say what you really feel only to someone who cares."

> *Roger*: Do you ever look back to what God seemed like to you a couple of months ago?
>
> *Mary*: Yes. It seems unreal. It has nothing to do with my life now.
>
> *Roger*: I wonder whether it might be worthwhile to recall it and spend some time with it?

One director has said of his own feelings in situations like this: "It is as though you have been walking together down a long, straight corridor. Then you turn a corner to find yourself suddenly confronted by a massive stone wall, with no door. You are keenly aware of the directee's frustration, and you yourself feel dispirited, afraid, and a little angry that your way has been so completely blocked."

Roger's feelings keep him sensitive to the intensity of Mary's frustration. He is also aware that, despite the intransigence of her feelings, she has a choice that she can make. She can choose to keep recalling her experience of God's care for her and her spontaneous openness to God. To recognize that she has a choice does not minimize its difficulty. But she can give attention to her memory of God's care, and she will not unless she decides to do so. If she does not make this choice, the memory will remain, like most memories, unavailable to contemplation.

Making this choice would be a major moment in the process of accepting God as God has shown Godself to be. It would allow the dialogue with God to proceed. If he remains faithful to his task of facilitation, Roger will not urge Mary to make the choice. He will, however, help her to keep the possibility of choice in mind, and to remain aware that she has not made it.

Mary's indecision has been brought about by a phenomenon that appears frequently through the course of spiritual life. We will call it "counter-movement." Counter-movement is an impulse, and counter-current a stream of recurrent impulses that prompt a person to withdraw from new life or the approach of new life. "Resistance" in psychology refers to analogous promptings.

In the event we have just described, Mary has withdrawn from the memory that God has cared for her and from the nascent realization that God may be caring for her still. The experience of knowing God's care and responding to it still attracts her, but the force of the impulse to withdraw makes consideration of the attraction a difficult, even a herculean, task.

The painful events that have occurred in Mary's family could well give her reason to think that God is arbitrary and callous. It is the inner event, however, that betrays the presence of counter-movement. Although she has recently been convinced by her experience of God that God cares for her, she behaves now as though that event had never occurred. To consider both the painful events in her family and her experience of God caring for her and decide that God might after all be only an uncaring guardian of law would be regressive, but it would not be irrational. It is in her return to her old perception of God without seriously considering her recent contrary experience of God that the impulse to stop her movement toward God potently reveals itself.

When a director encounters a prolonged and intense counter-movement in a directee, he—or she—can easily make the mistake of thinking the directee obtuse, or perversely acquiescing in his own unfreedom. The director can then become nonplussed or angry. Yet a counter-movement is inexplicable unless it is seen as the harbinger of new life. A counter-movement counters a movement toward freedom and toward God. If the director can ally himself with the possibility of new life and with the directee's freedom to make his own decisions he will want to remain in vital contact with the directee as the directee hesitates. Recalling how often he himself has resisted the approach of new life will be particularly helpful in enabling him to summon up the patience to do so. When a person deeply desires God, the defeats inflicted by counter-movement are likely to be only temporary.

The Basic Task Remains the Same

The process of direction takes place on the ground of the directee's life and prayer. It changes ground as the directee's life and relationship with God change. Today the ground on which direction takes place may be the directee's desire for more interior freedom. Next week it may be his resentment at a loss he has suffered. Six months from now it may be an attraction to Jesus as he appears in the gospel account of his meeting with the widow of Naim. Ten months from now it can be an attraction to Jesus' enthusiasm for the poor coupled with the directee's embarrassment when he himself is approached by beggars. Over months and years the ground changes as the directee's awareness and prayer change.

The director's basic task, however, will remain the same. It will always be the facilitation of the directee's encounter and dialogue with God. On whatever ground the dialogue with God takes place, the director will best serve the directee by helping him to become absorbed in what God is like and candidly express to God what he experiences as he stands before God.

The Effect of Fear on Direction

When people have had little or no experience of spiritual direction, they can enter into the process with some degree of fear:

> I was afraid that you were going to try to force me
> into a box, make me conform to particular stand-
> ards. It took awhile before I could relax and believe
> that was not going to happen to me. It was then
> that I could let the fist in my stomach unclench.

This fear urges a directee to defend himself and siphons off the energy that could be focused on relating to God.

Fear may be a result of a previous experience of direction. Another directee spoke of realizing that he was disappointing his director:

> Doris let me know that she had expected me to be
> further into prayer after three months of direction.
> I felt as though I had robbed her of all her Christ-
> mas presents!

Reactions such as these reinforce the need for the director to emphasize that there is no method to be learned and no specific goal to be reached. We try to help directees to remain open to God's action and to increase their awareness of what God seems to be doing and saying. We invite directees to continue the struggle to pray and to allow God to keep revealing Godself to them.

It is up to God to work directly with the praying person: inviting, challenging, consoling, revealing, and even at times demanding response. Recognizing God acting can also generate fear, but this fear is usually accompanied by attraction. It becomes the director's responsibility to encourage the directee to keep looking at and following God's leading, especially as the directee comes to recognize that there are no clear-cut rules that guarantee growth in relationship with God.

> I came to the Center thinking that I would get some answers, some signposts that would help me to see where God was calling me and what I ought to do. I believed that God would become crystal clear. Instead I kept finding that there were all kinds of surprises. Nothing worked the way I thought it was supposed to. As I look back now, I can see moments of joy and moments of pain. The only thing I am sure of now is that I can never be certain about what God is going to do. But God knows and I am going to keep letting myself be surprised, even when I don't particularly like it.

If then there is no method, no gauge to measure concretely either the amount or type of growth in relationship that will occur, directees are entitled to ask what they can rely on. Is there anything that will indicate what is likely to happen between God and the directee?

Relationship with God as a Dance

One way to look at the on-going relationship with God, the struggle between God and the directee to continue meeting each other, is to compare it to a dance. A man reading these pages may easily recall the anxiety he felt the first time he searched a dance floor for the person he most wanted to approach. He may also remember the sweaty palms, the wild beating of his heart, as he searched for the courage to risk the coldness of refusal and ask the woman to dance. A woman could be reminded of the apprehension she felt about not attracting a partner after hours of preparation and waiting. Her apprehension might have been immeasurably increased when she was approached by someone she did not know or someone who had little attraction for her. And it is not unheard of, although it is sometimes difficult to understand, that a woman will refuse to dance with the person for whom she feels the most attraction.

Many of these feelings and reactions are also apparent when God first approaches a directee. God stands before the person waiting for a sign of recognition, hoping for an indication of welcome and acquiescence. The dance can begin or not, depending on the response of the other. This is what we can often forget when we look at the relationship with God. God does take the initiative, but we can and do say no as often as we say yes.

If there is a positive response, then the dance can begin. In our fantasies, of course, we move into a dance exactly as did Fred Astaire and Ginger Rogers, or Gene Kelly and Leslie Caron. There is no faltering, no testing, no mistake. But we all know that this is seldom true in the reality of life. Dancing requires learning and practice. The steps may be simple but they are also intricate, and the tricky dimension is that I not only have to learn the movement and mood of my own body but also the movement and mood of my partner's. There is dependence on the other at all times if we are to have a partnership, a common venture, a task to be shared as well as joy in the sharing.

The two people must learn to move together in harmony, with a sense of suppleness and lightness. We have two very individual people who achieve a sense of at-oneness only through work and practice.

In the dance there are moments when the two separate and move away from each other. If the dance is to continue, the partners have to be intent on turning again toward each other, a swift looking, a refinding, then achieving grace and harmony again. In the same way, if the relationship with God is to be continued, the two remain conscious of each other with all that this implies: seeking, asking again, accepting, and moving together.

In the dance there is continuous movement, constant searching out. There are moments of anxiety and other moments of fluid joy and supple grace. The question of who does the leading becomes purely a technical one. There is a mutuality of relationship, a desire to blend and to meld as one. The true dancer knows through experience that the secret of mutuality lies in trust, suppleness, sensitivity to the slightest rhythmic motion of the partner. Does this say anything about the relationship we seek with God?

The first moment is one that can never be recaptured. It happens once and only once. Those of us who have experienced God's invitation recognize this moment for ourselves. It is that time when we finally say our yes with a full heart, despite our fear that we will not know the right steps, that we will not know how to follow, or indeed not even be sure that we want to follow. But we say yes and the dance begins.

Until that happens, we are like the people in the Samaritan village who came out to see Jesus because the sinful woman claimed to have talked to one who was more than the ordinary traveler. It was only when they made the effort to hike out to the well and experienced him talking directly to each of them that they could say: "We believe now, not because of what you have told us, but because we have seen and heard him ourselves."

In the ongoing relationship we rely on this first experience of dancing with God, but we cannot remain there. God is constantly calling on us to learn new moods, new rhythms, new steps. If we wish to become proficient, we set ourselves to the task. The struggle, the exercise, the practice may be somewhat daunting at times, but each new dance will find us more flexible, more supple, more filled with grace.

Chapter 7

Supervision at the Center

Supervision, a hallmark of the associates' program, is a procedure that encourages exploration and reflection. Supervisor and associate explore together and reflect on the associate's ability to facilitate the directee's growth. The process helps associates to become clearer about the presuppositions and feelings they bring to direction that can slow down, and sometimes block, the development of a directee's prayer. The process also encourages reflection on positive qualities that enhance the direction, enabling the associate to ponder the question: "What is it in me that helps the person to keep up a momentum to pray and to talk about that prayer?" It is the practical experience of the associate that is supervised. Supervision is rooted in what is actually being done and not in what is being studied. The following example will illustrate what supervision is like.

A directee has said:

> I was very angry with my wife last week. She went shopping and left our children in a neighbor's care, promising to be back by 3:30. When I arrived home at 4:30, I found Mrs. Olsen very angry because Alice wasn't back and she'd had to rearrange all her own plans. I tried to placate her but was upset myself at Alice's lateness. Alice didn't get back until 5:30 and couldn't understand what all the fuss was about. We had a fight to end all fights. (Pause) Since then, I have not been able to concentrate on my prayer at all.

> *Director*: That's too bad. I can tell that you are upset.
> Has this kind of thing happened before?

A supervisor could react to the director's response in several ways. Here are a couple of possibilities. The supervisor could say:

> You are asking a factual question here. It's the kind
> of question that will lead you to look more deeply
> into the problem. What you should have done in-
> stead is stay with the prayer and ask your directee
> to stay with it, too.

Such a response might help a director to know better what to say and do in similar situations in the future. It would not, however, help the director to reflect on why he chose to concentrate on the marital dispute and overlook what the directee said about his prayer. The supervisor might also say:

> Your directee told you about his anger. Did you no-
> tice that he seemed to be saying all this about his
> wife in order to lead up to a statement about his
> prayer? I wonder why you missed that? Maybe we
> need to look at who needed to talk about the prob-
> lem—you or he?

This second response will lead to conversation that is fo-cused on a choice the director has made and his reasons for making that choice. It is this kind of help the supervisor is called upon to give. Looking at *why* enables the director to gain greater clarity about the relationship. It also enables the director to move toward a more directly helpful interaction with the directee.

Supervision and Instruction

The difference between instruction and supervision can be compared on one level to the difference in carpentry between the instruction manual included in a "Do-it-yourself" kit and the assistance given by an experienced advisor. The kit supplies the necessary parts. The manual recommends appropriate tools, tells the practioner how to use them, and instructs him in the assembly and finishing of his product. The carpenter feels ready to begin.

Putting the parts together can be another matter, however. "It looked so simple!" the carpenter may moan as he struggles with wooden and metal parts, tools, screws, holes, and instructions. At this juncture he takes one of several steps: he may get exasperated enough to throw the kit into the trash; he may set it aside for another day that probably will never come; or he may look for someone experienced enough to help him complete his task satisfactorily.

In this process the carpenter has had two distinct and different experiences. Both are necessary, but they are not the same. Instructions give us the facts, but experience shows us how to put what we know into action. Supervision, that is, consultation with a reflective and more experienced person, helps us to avoid or correct errors. Supervision enables us to move through difficulties and frustrations without yielding to the temptation to believe ourselves defeated. Supervision also offers hope and encouragement for future endeavors.

On just about every level other than the one we have just exemplified, becoming more fully a spiritual director is a different process from becoming more fully a carpenter. In this respect, however, they are alike. An associate attends classes devoted, for instance, to the exposition of religious experience. Religious experience is defined, its characteristics are clearly identified, and copious notes are taken. Examples of religious experience are given, some quite obvious, others surprising. The teacher might assign books and articles referring to the essential qualities and significance of religious experience and the associate director is called upon to compare, analyze and assess the differences brought out by the various authors. Associates are asked to write a paper about one of their own religious experiences or one that has been described to them in spiritual direction. Further classes focus on how to help a person describe and contemplate a religious experience. Class response and interaction are stimulating and enthusiastic.

Several days later, an associate discusses a report on a direction session with a supervisor. A religious experience virtually leaps off the page, yet the associate might miss it entirely! Or he or she might advert to it and then move at once to another subject. The class work, then, has not provided the associate with the ability to get absorbed in the person's experience long enough to hear it and talk about it. It is through the combination of classwork and supervision that theory and practice begin to come together. Supervision is never just casual chatting, even chatting about what is going on in direction. It is a serious attempt to help directors move from knowledge about spiritual direction to being absorbed in the experience of directees who are trying to be absorbed in God. It is an effort to move from "how to" to "why."

Associates' Reactions to Supervision

Each full-time staff member at the Center supervises two or three associates weekly. Each associate receives two hours of individual supervision, either in one session or in two one-hour sessions. Before the program begins, many applicants say that they are looking forward to supervision.

Following are comments that we have heard from applicants:

I've had some training, but mostly in the form of workshops. I want to pull all that knowledge together, and make some connecting links because I do feel a need for continuity. I think the Center will provide that. The other thing that attracts me is being supervised in the work I do here.

Good supervision will help me to develop a greater trust in what I have learned in the past . . . I've looked carefully at several other programs that offer what appears to be excellent theory.

I certainly don't know everything about spiritual direction, but I believe the time is right for me to get as much supervision as I can. In other words, I need someone who will help me to look at what I'm actually doing and to become the best director I can be. . . .

I've had several years of experience in doing spiritual direction. I know that I've been helpful to people and I have received a lot of affirmation. There are times, however, when I'm aware that I'm not listening carefully enough. A few times I've experienced boredom, even though the person is not boring. I'm sure that good supervision can help me to look at experiences like those and help me to see what's going on beneath the surface. . . .

Many associates, then, look forward to supervision when they begin the program. Despite the staff's efforts to make the purpose and focus of supervision clear in the admissions interview, however, associates can begin supervision without a clear perception of how it works and what it is intended to accomplish. Some still expect that the major emphasis will be placed on providing them with helping techniques.

Rosalie, for example, is working with a directee who does not seem able to pray. Rosalie might anticipate at the start of the program that her supervisor will offer her some specific questions for the directee to answer about his prayer. She may look forward to the supervisor's selection of "right" passages from scripture for the directee. She may visualize the supervisor as analyzing the problem for her so that she will know in which direction to lead the directee. If this were so, the steps in the supervisory process would be simple. Rosalie would be taught and would assimilate what she had been taught. She would then apply it.

Supervision at the Center does not exclude the practical helps just cited but it moves a long step beyond. The emphasis is quite different and calls for a totally different set of responses from directors. The directors are working with people who are searching for a more personal God. Their task is to help directees come to a more active awareness of God, to react to that awareness, to share those reactions with God, and to wait for God's response. It stands to reason that directors can accomplish this adequately only if they are able to deal with their own lives, their own prayer, and their own deepest feelings.

Rosalie, and others like her, may initially be disappointed. It is not unusual for an associate to become angry and accusatory: "You never tell me what to do. All you ever do is ask me questions." It takes time, energy, and experience for an associate to recognize that further development for a spiritual director means entering more fully into a way of life, not learning a new set of methods and techniques.

The supervisor helps associates to become more aware of what is going on in them as they listen to directees. Directees talk about their lives, prayer, and relationship with God. How does this affect a director? Do his reactions move him toward engagement and involvement with another's life? Or do they distance him from what is happening to the directee?

Recognizing and Reacting to God

One of the principal difficulties for a director is recognizing and reacting to God's movement in a person's life. A directee may come for direction conscious that God has been present to her in a personal way and has been saying something to her though nature, people, events, or scripture. Even though the directee knows that something important has happened, she is likely to introduce the subject with self-deprecating remarks such as, "You'll think I'm crazy, but . . ." She may downplay what happened by saying, "My imagination was probably working overtime and I was tired." She may sound vague and confused about God's action: "It seemed as though God was close but as I look back on it now, I can't remember clearly and I wonder if it really did happen."

The supervisor recognizes remarks like these when she sees them written in a report. Her own experience as a spiritual director has taught her how hesitant a directee can be to accept the possibility that God is acting in her.

The supervisor knows too that the director's response can influence the directee's view of the credibility of the experience and her willingness to talk further about it. Consider the responses two different directors might make.

One director, Joe, might say:

> Crazy? You know you've said that before. I remember a few weeks ago when you had that quarrel with your mother because you were so tired. Have you been getting enough sleep lately?

Another director, Rita, might comment:

> Sometimes when a person has an experience of God it helps to write it down. You could try that next time so that when you come for direction we can talk about it.

The first response invites the directee to focus on her anxiety. The second tells the directee what to do the *next* time God comes close. But what has happened to God in the experience? Somehow God has been shunted aside. We could, with a little imagination, picture God saying woefully: "Director, I was counting on you to help, not hinder me."

A supervisor would ask the director whether he noticed what God was doing in the directee's experience. If he did not notice it, what was going on in him that kept him from noticing? Was *he* tired? Bored? Distracted? Fearful?

Was he aware of anything happening in him at that moment? If he says that indeed he did hear the person say that God had seemed close, the supervisor will want to know what prompted him to move away from what was going on in the directee's prayer.

Responses usually sound something like this:

Joe: I wanted her to recognize that she wasn't crazy. I thought maybe it was just her imagination but I didn't want to say that, so I grabbed onto the word "tired."

Rita: I thought if she couldn't remember it clearly, and doubted it, that we'd be wasting our time trying to recall something so vague. But I also wanted to help her remember so that she could be clearer the next time.

Each director is, after all, a human being who is experiencing a number of feelings. The first reaction to the supervisor's questions is likely to be as defensive as that of a goose protecting her goslings. In addition to dealing with whatever feelings caused the director to move away from the religious experience, the supervisor will also have to help the director work through this defensiveness.

When Rita and Joe have had time to reflect further on their reactions, they might say:

I feel as though I'd be invading her privacy. After all, this is holy ground.

A director shouldn't be pushing someone to talk about her experiences with God. I think she'd tell me if she really wanted me to know.

You've been telling me that I should help directees to recognize and stay with their feelings. That's what I'm doing here.

Over and over the supervisor asks: "What were you feeling when she told you that she felt God was close?" Eventually the director begins to name whatever the feeling was: fear of the experience in itself, fear of not asking the right questions, irritation because the directee seemed vague, resentment because the director himself has not felt God close for some time, doubt that the experience was real, or annoyance be-

cause he thought that the directee had not really been praying. An exhaustive list of the feelings that could arise and an
adequate account of the perceptions that might prompt them
would run on indefinitely. Once the director comes to understand what prompted him to overlook or avoid the religious
experience, however, he has something concrete to work with.
Slowly he can allow himself to acknowledge the feelings as
they become evident to him. Once he acknowledges them, he
can begin to learn through experience how to prevent them
from being an obstacle to the directee's developing relationship with God.

Recognizing movements can be another area of difficulty
for the director. When we speak of movements here, we are
referring to whatever inner impulse seems to be leading the
person toward or away from God and God's action. The supervisor's task is to help the director to perceive these impulses
clearly. The difficulty the director encounters may be a simple
matter of not listening attentively. It can also be a tendency to
be selective in her hearing. She may be so eager to help that
she fastens onto the first thing she hears and then stops listening. Her attention is focused on what she will say to the
directee about the first part of his account so she fails to notice other reactions he mentions. She thus loses the thread
that indicates that the directee is experiencing more than one
movement. An example will illustrate this. Frank, who has
come for direction to Melanie for several months, describes an
incident that occurred while he was praying.

> *Frank*: I was praying on a favorite scripture passage last
> week. It's in Mark, the passage in which Jesus sent
> the disciples out two by two. After they returned he
> invited them to go off with him to a lonely place. Im-
> mediately I felt a kind of warmth and longing. I felt as
> though I was being invited, too . . .
>
> *Melanie*: It sounds as though you were really captivated
> by that invitation. . . .

Frank: I was (he smiles). But a lonely place . . . I'm not keen on lonely places.

Melanie can now invite Frank to talk further about the warmth and longing, the attraction—what seems to be leading him toward God. In doing so she will serve Frank well because she will be inviting him to explore a movement toward God.

If Frank concentrates only on the invitation, however, Melanie is likely to find that the conversation will soon peter out. For Frank has more on his mind than Jesus' invitation. He has told Melanie about his reaction to the loneliness of the place, and for all Melanie knows the reaction may have been strong. His reaction could also indicate that he is afraid to be alone with Jesus. If this happens it will be important for Melanie's supervisor to help her see that more was occurring than she seemed to recognize. If she truly wants to be of as much assistance to Frank as she can be, Melanie will have to become more engaged with Frank and *all* the experience he recounts.

The Director's Feelings

There is a possibility that something else is going on in Melanie, something that could lead her in either of two directions. Neither of these would be of service to Frank or to God. One direction in which Melanie could go would be dictated by some of her own hidden feelings. Supervision can help her to discover and deal with them. In our experience we have seen some directors fasten like limpets on the positive feelings indicated by a directee, effectively banishing from their consciousness any feelings that have a negative tone. In such cases, they will hear only what is encouraging, and will tend themselves to resort to time-tested clichés such as "God is good," "God loves us," "We can only see what God is doing through faith," and "God writes straight with crooked lines." Underneath such statements their own anxiety may be at work. If they have not resolved some of their personal problems of relationship with God, they cannot become engaged with the struggles a directee may encounter in meeting God.

Other directors are persistent searchers in the dark places of the spirit. They are at home in the dismal atmosphere of the storm. They have had tender experiences of God, but more readily recall the experiences of life that have caused them pain. Although God is sometimes revealed to them as loving, tender, and caring, they forget those experiences and spontaneously react with doubt and distrust. These personal feelings keep them captive and unable to hear others' experience of God acting in their lives.

It can happen that they are keenly aware of their darker feelings. They sense that they are being controlled by their own angers, fears, jealousies, or lack of self-worth. However, they feel incapable of facing these feelings in their own prayer. They can believe that in helping others to face darkness, they will overcome darkness in themselves. In such situations directors rely on the directee's strength rather than their own. This role reversal calls for immediate help in supervision. Both supervisor and director need to grapple with whatever feelings the director experiences that keep her or him from engaging with all the feelings the directee brings to direction. The director must come to an inner freedom that will enable her to encourage the same freedom in the directee.

The director must actively believe that warmth, tenderness, discomfort and fear can be channeled into growth in the relationship with God. All these feelings that could lead the directee toward or away from God are necessary for the spiritual journey.

No feeling is worthless; all of them express the reality of the person. Some feelings often give an impetus toward God. Some feelings show directees what impedes the movement toward God and prompt them to make a conscious choice.

Directors cannot facilitate growth if they have not struggled to grow themselves and if they do not believe growth in relationship with God is worth the struggle. The supervisor's task is difficult and sometimes arduous. It is also extremely rewarding. In our example the supervisor must help Melanie to realize, if she does not already know it, that Frank is expressing attraction but is also expressing some reluctance. The supervisor and director then have to work together to discover the underlying feelings in Melanie that hinder Frank's recognition of his own movements toward and away from God. Melanie's increasing freedom can, indirectly at least, enhance Frank's freedom. When Melanie can say to Frank, "You felt warmth and longing when Jesus seemed to be inviting you. But then you seemed a little hesitant. Maybe you could say more about those different feelings," she will be listening and reacting fully to him. She will also be respecting Frank, who obviously wanted her to hear both his reactions. Through Melanie's comment Frank is now told that it is all right to have different and contrasting reactions. He will thus be invited to keep on being candid and to explore how these reactions affect his relationship with God.

A particularly troublesome area is the difficulty a director can experience in interacting with a directee's more intense feelings. People often find it especially hard to name and express these feelings. Some directees have learned to consider certain feelings acceptable—enthusiasm, glee, courage, peace—but consider it unacceptable to acknowledge boredom, envy, terror, or jealousy. Directees experiencing such feelings and unable to express them often arouse reactions of anger, pity, frustration, even helplessness in the director. Conversation can flow smoothly between them until the intense feeling is experienced. Then the directee goes mute or falls back on platitudes such as "God knows what he's doing" or opaque remarks like "The person I'm working with is undisciplined and short-tempered, but I keep being nice to him and try to put up with it," or "My father never had any time for me or any interest in me, but he was a good man and I learned not to need what he couldn't give." Some directors accept these statements at face value and may not try to help the directee to see whether anger, hurt, or rejection lurks behind them. As a result, nothing happens in the direction. A plateau is reached, and both directee and director walk around and around on the plateau without making any forward movement. A sense of apathy, boredom, or frustration slowly builds up and the director wonders how they have come to this impasse.

On the other hand, some directees give the appearance of constantly teetering on the edge of a semiactive volcano. What would cause a mild reaction in others evokes fire and flame in them. They are seldom irritated but often furious. They are rarely fond of but usually care intensely about whoever or whatever attracts their attention for the moment. They are fascinated by their own feelings and frequently display an inner force in expressing them that is capable of hypnotizing their audience. Directors who fall under their spell will usually find, after the directee has gone, that they are left frustrated and confused. The ease with which the directee has controlled the focus and flow of the conversation makes the director wonder whether he will ever be able to engage the directee in a give-and-take discussion.

Each situation will elicit a unique mixture of reactions in a director. It will also bring about a unique interaction with the directee. One fact remains constant: in each situation the director does react. He must become aware of his reactions and learn to put them at the service of the directee's growth.

A supervisor helps a director to interact with the intensity of a directee's feelings by noting the feelings with him, and by questioning and challenging him as well as supporting him. Challenge will often be necessary if the director is to reach the awareness he will need in order to help the directee to grow in awareness. When, for example, a director is bored because the directee expresses little feeling, the supervisor begins by reflecting carefully on a report of part of a conversation with the director. An excerpt from the dialogue could look like this:

Ed (the director): You were saying that your prayer was O.K. this week. Do you mean you enjoyed it, or that it was pretty routine?

Kathy: It was good. I read the story of Jesus curing the ten lepers. I thought a lot about Jesus' power to heal. And I do like the healing miracles.

Ed: Was there anything in particular that you noticed? Anything that meant something significant to you?

Kathy: Not really. I'm one of the healed, but there wasn't anything momentous.

Ed then notes: "I can't recall much more about the interview except the realization that I'm a little frustrated. I do like Kathy. She is a fine person but we don't seem to be going anywhere and I need some help. My question for supervision is: What can I do to help Kathy get more out of her prayer?

The supervisor sees that Ed needs to look at his relationship with Kathy and his feeling of frustration.

Joe (the supervisor): Let me ask you a couple of questions. First, I noticed that you said you were a little frustrated. How frustrated were you really? A little? A lot?

Ed: I wasn't angry.

Joe: You weren't angry. You're telling me what you weren't. Can you tell me what you were? For instance, if you felt free to say exactly what you were feeling, what would you have said?

Ed: I guess I felt like telling her to go home and come back when she had more to say.

Joe: But you weren't angry.

Ed: Well, I wasn't in a rage or anything like that.

Joe: How have you felt the last couple of times when you knew Kathy was coming? Did you feel good about seeing her? Did you have a sinking feeling? Or what?

    Ed: I need a minute to try to recall . . . I have to admit I
      felt a little down, a bit as though we're not going any-
      where.

As the conversation continues Ed begins to unearth some
deeper feelings of discouragement. At first, these center on
Kathy. Perhaps she is not ready for spiritual direction,
perhaps she does not want a deeper relationship with God,
perhaps she is too much "in her head" for direction. The supervisor listens, but eventually asks:

    Joe: What about you? I hear you analyzing what may be
      wrong with Kathy. But you're the one who is frus-
      trated and discouraged. How are you feeling about
      yourself? And about yourself as a director?

    Ed: Not good at all. I'm wondering why I can't help her. I
      know I'm doing well with other directees but there's a
      block with Kathy.

The director may well discover as he continues to talk that he
likes Kathy too much to be fully objective about her. He does
not want her to be hurt. He is too protective of her. He may
realize that he finds it difficult to work with people who cannot express their deep feelings. It could be that she reminds
him of his own difficulties in praying. Whatever else he becomes aware of, he must discover what is at the root of his
own feelings of discouragement if he is to develop a more
genuinely receptive attitude toward her. For the purposes of
this example, we will assume that Ed begins to realize that he
is afraid that nothing significant is going to happen and that
he will fail Kathy. He starts to recognize his fear of his own
inadequacy. The supervisor is able then to take Ed back to the
report. They discuss how Ed's fear of his own inadequacy af-
fects his spiritual direction sessions with Kathy. If we turn for
a moment from the conversation between Ed and Joe to look
again at what Kathy said to Ed, we notice a progression from
"Jesus' power to heal" to "I do like the healing miracles . . ."

and then to "I'm one of the healed. . . ." Now we can turn back to Ed and Joe.

> *Joe*: Ed, did you notice what Kathy was saying about the healing? Let's take a look at that. Would you read what she said out loud and listen?
>
> Ed does so, pauses, and then says:
> "I'm one of the healed." That's powerful, isn't it? How come I just heard flatness?

After further exploration of Kathy's statements and Ed's reactions to them, the supervisor and Ed turn to the effect Ed's reactions have had on Kathy. Ed has to take this one incident and ask himself how his expectation that nothing was going to happen in Kathy's prayer has adversely affected Kathy. He also has to ask himself how similar expectations may have affected other directees in the past. Ed will then have to discover in his own reflection and prayer how to deal with his fear of his own inadequacy.

Both Ed and Joe are aware that in the meantime Ed still has a continuing direction relationship with Kathy and that his responsibility to her is of paramount importance. A directee cannot wait for the resolution of the director's difficulties before continuing the development of her own relationship with God. It is vitally important that Ed, despite his own limitations, be able to encourage Kathy to become more deeply engaged in prayer. It has been our experience that directors, when they have brought their own reactions to consciousness and begun to reflect, pray about them, and talk freely to a supervisor, have been able to encourage directees in Kathy's situation. The director will be all the more likely to offer helpful encouragement if he or she realizes that God is more engaged with a directee's growth than he himself can ever be. God wants something to happen in direction that will be freeing and creative for the directee. This means that God will be working too.

Acknowledging that God is placing a great deal of trust in him can also be a source of strength and freedom for the director. Sobering and even frightening though this conviction can be, it can also enable him to become more engaged with what is happening to the directee without undue concern about his own struggles and fears. Ed, for example, may find himself reminding Kathy that she told him she was one of the healed. He may ask her if she has a reaction to that assertion. He can show his interest in her prayer. He can be gentle but persistent until Kathy is free enough to allow herself to notice that she does have a reaction. He could suggest that it might be helpful for her to share that reaction with God and to ask God what it means to God. As Kathy pursues her own courageous venture, Ed experiences firsthand what can happen to a directee when the director is supportive. Vestiges of his own sense of inadequacy may remain, but they are likely gradually to lose their grip and no longer control Ed's actions.

The Director's Expectations

Associates are inclined to believe that they are equally accepting of and engaged with everyone they direct. "I like them all" is more often than not their spontaneous reply to the question "How do you feel about them?" All of us, however, are influenced by preconceived ideas and values when we meet new acquaintances and encounter new experiences. These preconceptions often lead to misconceptions which can influence and control our reactions. These misconceptions are insidious enemies of truth because they often work undetected or only partially perceived. And because they are so subtle, they can result in a lack of openness to anyone who is markedly different from the people with whom we readily associate. In the ministry of direction, they lead to assumptions about the other that prevent interest, engagement, and careful listening.

One of the supervisor's tasks is to notice any marked preference an associate shows toward some directees and any lack of attentiveness he or she shows toward others. How these attitudes affect the director's work will be of particular concern to the supervisor. Following is an example.

George, an associate, is a religious brother belonging to a congregation whose chief ministry is teaching in high schools. Eight people come to George for spiritual direction. He does not feel that he has any favorites among them.

After six weeks of supervision Emily, George's supervisor, notices that he has discussed the work he has done with six of his directees but has not mentioned two others at all. One is a woman religious and the other is a 35-year-old laywoman. Emily asks George how they are coming along in direction:

George: Fine. They're not having any problems at all.

Emily: Are they both praying?

George: I think as well as they can.

Emily: As well as they can? What does that mean?

George explains that both women are indeed praying but that he experiences a sense of sameness when the sister, Pat, speaks of prayer. She tends to generalize and George finds it hard to help her to be more concrete. She does not seem to expect much of herself. He feels that perhaps she is unable to do more. She seems satisfied with the direction, however, so George believes he should be satisfied too and not push Pat beyond her capabilities. Emily then asks about Marie, the laywoman. Does George experience sameness with her?

George: No, I'm not bored at all. She's very intriguing, as a matter of fact. There's a lot about her that I don't understand.

Emily: How come you haven't talked about your work with her? It sounds as though that might be helpful.

George tells Emily that Marie speaks of God and prays to God as mother and female friend. George has refrained from discussing this practice because he does not know what his theological stance should be. He feels that there is a lot going on in Marie, but he wants to give her more time to develop at her own pace and to feel at ease with him.

In situations in which the director perceives little movement in a directee's relationship with God and for one reason or other has not invited the directee to frank discussion about it, the supervisor knows that the directee may be saying more about himself or herself, or about his or her relationship with God, than the director realizes. The directee, for instance, may be asking for help without being heard. With such a possibility in mind, Emily asks George to prepare for their next supervisory session by writing a report on his most recent interview with each of these women. In their next session Emily discovers, and enables George to discover, that it is not Sister Pat whose expectations are low, but George's. He tells Emily that Pat reminds him of sisters who worked with him on a school faculty. They seemed to him "perfect and untouchable." "Self-satisfied," George characterizes them. "They had all the answers." George is surprised at the strength of his feelings when he talks about them. As the conversation continues, he is dismayed to realize that he has seen Pat as a replica of those sisters and has paid little attention to her as a person. He has categorized Pat and does not have much hope for her. The next time George meets Pat, he is able to listen to her as an individual person. He then discovers her uniqueness and her genuine desire to encounter God. He is amazed at her perseverance and delighted with her sense of humor. He is chagrined at his own previous lack of perception, but exhilarated to discover a new sense of freedom growing within himself.

Emily also looks at George's report on Marie. Marie is not engaging George in theological confrontation; rather, she seems to be asking for some encouragement, some sign from George that it is acceptable to pray as a woman to a woman.

The report shows that each time she mentions praying to God as mother, George changes the subject. Further discussion reveals that George has dismissed feminists as women to avoid. Because he is tentative and fearful in his relationship with Marie, she is becoming more tentative and fearful. George has been sliding away from what he has envisioned as debate. He has neglected to ask himself, "What is God trying to say to Marie?" As George struggles against his misconceptions, the supervisor is hopeful that George will help Marie in her struggle to relate to God as God wants Marie to relate.

The Use of the Focusing Paper in Supervision

It can be helpful occasionally for associates to give their supervisor an overall view of all the spiritual direction they are giving. However, supervisors can give concrete help only when the associate describes specific situations. It is through focusing on particular interchanges between directee and director, as far as the director can recall them, that the supervisor can help the director to notice what is really going on in the director and between the directee and the director.

At least six times a semester, then, directors give their supervisor a partial description of a conversation with a directee, usually one that raises issues about the quality of his or her work in the particular situation. It can also exemplify more general issues concerning the work that cause the director some degree of doubt or confusion. Because the description enables the director and supervisor to focus on one aspect of the director's work, it is called a focusing paper.

The supervisor always has the welfare of the directee in mind. Code names are used in focusing papers to protect his or her privacy. The supervisor frequently asks: "What did this person come for? Is the person getting what she or he came for?" However, the supervisor focuses primarily on the director's reactions. This focus reveals the quality of the interchange and often provides a starting point for discussion of the director's attitude toward the directee and what he or she has said. Jeanne, for example, feels frustrated because she is not able to help Mark pray. A part of her focusing paper sounds like this:

Mark: Jeanne, this has not been the best of weeks for me. It seems as though everything I've been involved in has gone wrong.

Jeanne: Sounds bad . . . what happened?

Mark: Well, I was dumbfounded on Tuesday. It seems that my wife, Gen, has been wanting to buy a stove for some time. She mentioned it again and was furious when I said I didn't see how we could afford it. I just hadn't realized how long she's been waiting for it. I felt horrible about it.

Jeanne: She sounds upset. I hope you were able to talk it out. What else happened last week?

Mark: My work situation has been quite tense. It's budget time, and there have been a few layoffs, so everyone is on edge. I had done my usual report, but for some reason the division manager got angry and left it on my desk with a curt note. When I tried to talk to him about it later on, he refused to discuss it. He was very controlled, icy. I felt terrible about it and really confused, like a kid in school who's been reprimanded but doesn't know why.

Jeanne: It has been a bad week for you.

Jeanne tells her supervisor that she is frustrated and angry because Mark does nothing but complain. Yet she cannot help him to take his difficulties to God in prayer. When Jeanne suggested that he try to tell God what the week was like for him, Mark seemed disinclined to do so. Jeanne wonders why her suggestion leaves him indifferent.

The supervisor notices almost immediately that Mark, as he described his reactions, used strong feeling words: "dumb-

founded," "horrible," "terrible," "confused." He describes himself as feeling "like a kid in school who's been reprimanded
and doesn't know why." The supervisor also pays attention to
Jeanne's bland responses: "bad," "upset." She asks Jeanne
what is going on in her that keeps her from responding adequately to Mark. This lack of response, which would not have
been nearly as obvious in a more general discussion with her
supervisor, stands out clearly in the report.

A Collaborative Venture

Genuine supervision is a collaborative venture. Often a
director finds as she prepares her verbatim that recalling and
writing down what she remembers proves to be a powerful
instrument for her growth. She notices her own feelings. She
begins to ask herself why she ignored a particular comment.
She becomes aware, perhaps, that she is pushing the directee,
leading or advising, and not listening. When the supervisory
session begins, the director is prepared to initiate the discussion.

Collaboration becomes much more difficult when the director, after writing the focusing paper and reflecting on it,
still does not realize what has been happening. The supervisor
then has to help the director to reflect on each response in the
relevant part of the focusing paper. This can be a slow and
painstaking process. The supervisor asks:

—What were you feeling when she said . . .?

—If you weren't aware of feeling anything then, how
did you react as you were writing the focusing paper?

—How are you feeling about it now?

—As you look at the dialogue now, do you have any
specific questions about anything you said?

—How would you respond now if you had a chance
to do the conversation over again?

—Do you see what you did (how you reacted) when
the directee began to speak about . . .?

Sometimes such questioning fails to elicit helpful reflection from the director. The supervisor might then role-play
the pertinent part of the report with him or her. In our example, the supervisor asks Jeanne to read Mark's part of the dialogue and as she reads, to try to let herself feel the feelings he
expressed. After completing the role play, Jeanne jots down
how she felt. It now becomes obvious to Jeanne that Mark
experienced deep emotions. Although she heard his words, she
did not recognize the strength of his feeling until she tried to
get inside his skin. She realizes now that her "bad" response
to his "terrible" must have communicated to him that she considered his feelings unimportant.

During Mark's next conversation with her, Jeanne notices a definite difference both in herself and in him. When
she reacts strongly to a feeling he expresses, he is able to say
more to her. Before the end of their conversation, he refers to
childhood experiences of feeling unloved. Eventually, Mark is
able to speak to God about his fears. When he does, he finds
God both understanding and comforting. His relationship
with God begins to develop. He comments to Jeanne that he is
also noticing changes in his relationships with significant people in his life.

In the meantime, the supervisor continues her work with
Jeanne. She encourages Jeanne to concentrate on the sections
of her reports that show her overlooking her own feelings, as
well as those of directees. Jeanne begins to recognize her own
fears and anxieties. As she does, she becomes better able to
hear what directees say and to react to them even when their
feelings arouse anxiety in her.

A major task of the supervisor is to help a director to
interact with each person differently, as God does. Some directors seem not to realize that God sees each person as
unique and moves uniquely into the experience of each one.
A director's own experience of God cannot serve as a paradigm

of relationship with God. It is only one of an infinite variety of ways in which God interacts with people.

A supervisor often has to help a director relate to the dynamic of what happens with God rather than to the details. Tony, for example, has been receiving spiritual direction for a few months. One day he tells Mike, his director, that several times when he was praying Jesus seemed very close and seemed to show Tony his Sacred Wounds. Tony is deeply moved and believes that Jesus is asking him to be more compassionate toward others. Since these prayer experiences, Tony has been able to curb his impatience toward several of his co-workers. Two of them have even remarked on the difference they have noticed in him.

Mike listens as Tony describes these experiences and then, his focusing paper shows, abruptly changes the subject. The supervisor's inquiries reveal that Mike himself sees Jesus as a companion. His older brother has often encouraged and supported Mike in his efforts to help others. Mike has often thought that Jesus' way with him was very similar. He has never had the impression that Jesus wanted him to contemplate his physical suffering. It was his dependable love, not his suffering, that Jesus wanted him to contemplate. Mike finds Tony's concentration on the Sacred Wounds morbid. As the supervisor continues to draw him out, Mike becomes aware that he does not believe Tony's "visions" and finds that kind of devotion repugnant.

A supervisor helps a director to respect God's freedom and ability to reveal Godself in the way that means most to each person. A directee's experience of life and people, his education, and the culture from which he comes give him a particular orientation toward life. God will ordinarily make use of that orientation to draw the person to Godself. Tony is touched deeply by the Sacred Wounds. God can use this attraction to speak the message of compassion to Tony.

A supervisor will help a director to look closely at this reality. The director should be encouraged to ask her or himself whether she wants a directee's relationship with God to be determined by what the director considers fitting or by what God and the directee deem appropriate. To help the director to look beyond his own devotional horizons, the supervisor might ask: "Has this experience effected a change in the directee's relationship with God?" If it has, the supervisor might then ask: "Has the change enabled the person to be more receptive to God?" He might continue with, "Are there results in the directee's life?" Even when an experience of God seems incongruous to a director, it can usually be trusted if it results in a stronger relationship with God and more genuinely loving attitudes toward other people. The action of God will identify itself by its consequences.

Mike has reason, then, to be supportive of Tony's experience of the Sacred Wounds. There is nothing morbid about becoming more patient and compassionate. Even if Tony still finds himself subject to bouts of impatience, there will be no reason to doubt his experience if he continues to struggle against them.

This difficulty manifests itself in many ways. Some directors become skeptical or inadvertently stop listening if a directee's experience as he or she describes it seems naive or old-fashioned. The same loss of attention or doubts can arise if an experience seems too light-hearted, if, for example, a directee envisions herself invited to dance before God or finds herself conversing with a Jesus who smiles a lot.

A supervisor does well to be alert for such reactions in a director. The supervisor can then help the director to look more closely at the experience and consider it in light of what God is accomplishing in the directee's prayer and life. If the relationship is developing, the director usually has reason to give careful attention to the experience as it is expressed in prayer.

The Associate's Reactions to Supervision

Individual supervision gives rise to a wide range of reactions in the director who is receiving it. An associate can find it painful to engage in such diligent examination of his ministry, particularly when the focus is fixed intently not only on what he is doing but also on why he is doing it. The very fact he is being supervised is challenging and supervision can often occasion feelings of tension, apprehension, fear and discouragement.

Fortunately, these are not the associate's only reactions to supervision. Quiet satisfaction in an increasing ability to help directees get what they came for is typically the dominant reaction to supervision. Moments occur when director and supervisor celebrate events that demonstrate dramatically a directee's entrance into a clear channel opening toward God. Elation and joy well up in them because this has happened and because they know that to a significant extent it has come about because of the director's inner freedom and ability to engage with the interaction between the directee and God.

Group Supervision

The insights and development of ability fostered in individual supervision are deepened and broadened in group supervision. Two or three times during the year, each associate has the opportunity to bring an example of his or her work in direction to the other associates and the staff for their observations and assistance.

Gen is troubled about her direction relationship with Al and about the quality of the work she is doing with him. She wants to find out whether her peers and the staff members see flaws in the way she relates to Al and to his experience of God. She would also like some concrete suggestions that will help her in future meetings with him.

Gen begins by sketching Al's background: his approximate age, his level of education, something of his occupation and religious background, his marital status, and his reason for asking for direction. For the sake of confidentiality, she omits any details that might identify him. For the same reason, she might alter some facts without, however, distorting her description or misleading her hearers.

Gen continues:

Al is pleasant, serious, and sincere. He speaks easily about his life and the people who are important to him. He claims that prayer is significant in his life. Every time I ask what's happening in his prayer, however, something changes between us. On the surface, Al still seems open and even affable, but the conversation flounders and he is unable to say anything that sounds real about his prayer. After consulting with my supervisor last week, I confronted Al with this perception. I told him he seemed to be blocking any discussion of prayer and that I found this puzzling.

He remained affable and relaxed, but I felt he tried to shift the responsibility over to me. I'd like to role-play that part of the conversation for you because I'm concerned about what went on between us. I have four questions I'd like you to bear in mind while you're listening:

—What do you see happening?

—What are your reactions?

—How do you feel I am responding to Al, his life and his prayer?

—Can you help me be of more help to him in his relationship with God?

Gen then presents, in the form of a role-play, a detailed account of part of her last meeting with Al. Another associate assists her by reading Al's part of the dialogue.

Gen begins by remarking that she waited for Al to start talking about his prayer. When he did not do so, she took the initiative:

Gen: Did you have anything you wanted to say about your prayer this week, Al?

Al: I'm still working at it. (He shrugs and is silent).

Gen: I'd like to talk more about your prayer, but first, let me ask you if you're satisfied with our times together so far. Are you finding them helpful?

Al (somewhat surprised): Why yes, particularly when I've been able to talk about some of the problems I've had with my family. I suppose you deal with so many directees that you find it difficult to recall.

Gen: I do remember, Al, and I'm glad that has been helpful. I have wondered about your prayer, though.

Al: But I've been talking about that with you too.

Gen: In a way you have, but I've been feeling uneasy and wanted to tell you.

Al: Uneasy? That surprises me, because I'm always relaxed when I'm here. I never would have guessed.

Gen: We talk easily together, Al, until prayer comes up, and then I sense you closing off.

Al: Why didn't you tell me that you were feeling like that?

Gen: I'm telling you now.

Al: I'm not closing off as far as I can tell. If you feel that way, I'm sorry, but all you have to do is ask. I will be glad to answer any questions when things aren't clear.

Gen: (At this point Al sits back in his chair rather deliberately and assumes a relaxed position. I become aware that I'm sitting forward with my hands clenched, so I try to relax too.)

Gen: Perhaps it would help, Al, if we went back to our last session together. Do you remember I suggested that you look at a passage of scripture and try to see what Jesus was like in that passage?

Al: Yes, I do. I was quite excited about it.

Gen: And do you remember that I suggested that you try to tell Jesus how you saw him and what that meant to you?

Al: I've tried to do that.

Gen: And do you remember that we agreed that you would try to tell me in direction how that prayer went for you, whether you were noticing anything new about Jesus or about yourself?

Al: Okay, I hear you. I thought I tried to do that, but it sounds as though I haven't succeeded. I will try again though, because I do want the spiritual direction, and I do want help with my prayer and my life.

Gen tells the group that Al cancelled his next meeting but left a message that he would come the following week. She talks about her frustration and anger at Al. She also feels guilty about the way she has been relating to him. She wonders whether he did talk about his prayer and, because it was not progressing as she wanted it to, she did not pay attention to him. She still feels, however, that Al was manipulating her and that he deliberately put her on the defensive.

The group reflects quietly for a few minutes, keeping Gen's questions in mind. Then each person in the group responds. One person comments that he found Gen tense and aggressive in the dialogue he heard. He felt she sounded accusatory and he wonders whether Al is afraid of displeasing her. Another says, "You were forthright and simple in telling Al how you felt initially, but then you got defensive. I felt annoyed toward the end of the dialogue. It sounded as though you were playing a game with one another."

Someone else is impressed by Al's sincerity. She wonders whether Gen should concentrate on helping him to pray instead of worrying about her performance. Yet another person felt sympathy for Al and wondered exactly what it was that was making Gen so angry and aggressive.

As people offer reactions, there is a growing agreement that there is forward movement in Al's response to direction. He has been able to talk about people and situations that are important to him and this has to be taken into account. The group believes that he does want to pray, and so they ask the question, "Is there something going on in you that makes you impatient with his attempts? Is it all right for Al to develop at his own pace, or does he have to move at yours?"

There is also some agreement that Al takes the offensive at times and at those times is probably trying to manipulate Gen. Some also wonder whether this might be because he is feeling unsure about himself, his prayer, his relationship with God, and his relationship with Gen. There is no attempt at this juncture to resolve Gen's difficulty, nor is there an attempt to come to consensus about the core of the problem. Gen and her supervisor note carefully what is said. After the meeting, they determine which observations seem most significant. Gen will then reflect further on the observations they have selected and will discuss the results of her reflection with her supervisor.

Advantages for the Associate Directors

There are definite advantages for the group through this process. The most obvious is the opportunity it affords associates to learn about direction situations they themselves have not yet encountered. The desire for God, with its strength and its ambivalence, comes to have many faces as they listen to one another's experiences. The action of God ceases to be abstract as it is seen finding its way into the experience of people they have never met and would not recognize if they did. The number of ways in which directors engage with directees' experience of their relationship with God becomes limitless as they listen. They will never encounter in their own ministry exactly the same situations they hear described, but what they hear expands their horizons, gives color and shape to new possibilities, and gradually helps them become more receptive to the situations they will encounter.

Another advantage is that the associates learn to talk objectively to colleagues about their ministry. Group supervision is an invaluable tool for helping directors become accustomed to asking for and receiving assistance from fellow ministers.

During the first months of the program, associates tend to support and encourage one another as much as they can. They hesitate to point out shortcomings in one another's work. This is to be expected as part of the process of coming to trust one another and to trust their own abilities as directors. Many directors, despite their previous experience, are nervous in the new environment of the Center, and need encouragement. Usually the trust level has risen by the second semester. Associates have become better able to listen receptively to comments that, though they remain encouraging and supportive, also contain elements of confrontation and challenge. When commenting on one another's work, associates are now more likely to remember that if they are to be genuinely helpful they must point out what they observe and say what they think, whether others approve or disagree. As a group they experience a keener desire to learn as much as possible.

Filtering

During the second half of the year, associates have also become more capable of filtering what they hear. They recognize more readily that some comments are pertinent and enlightening while others, though generally true, do not apply to this particular situation and this particular person. They are less defensive and less inclined to argue.

They are coming to learn that no one knows the solution to every difficulty. They listen with fewer biases and reflect more often on what is said. They are more confident that out of the comments and suggestions they hear they can select those that are helpful and let the rest go.

Advantages for Supervisors

Supervisors sometimes point without apparent result to an unproductive aspect of a direction relationship. The supervisor and the director try to understand what is happening, but the director does not seem to grasp the heart of the issue. Then the same director describes the relationship in group work. Someone in the group asks a question and light abruptly dawns. Many a supervisor has shaken her head in wry amusement at hearing her supervisee say to someone else, "I never thought of that. Thank you very much for your insight." A different approach has struck a chord the supervisor could not strike. If she is wise, the supervisor is grateful too.

The group may also notice something in the presentation that the presenter's supervisor has not seen. Her attention may have been directed too exclusively to another aspect of the relationship. A thoughtful supervisor will be the first to admit that the group can bring her to new insights and greater clarity. Finally, the fresh way a supervisor can listen as a member of the group can make her aware of something in the presentation that she has not noticed before.

Group work is, then, a genuine learning experience for staff members as well as associates.

How Development Becomes Apparent

As their year at the Center advances, associates as well as supervisors notice that the associates have changed. They speak more openly now about both their strengths and their weaknesses. They learn to rely on their strengths and use them more actively and confidently in direction. They come to grips with traits that make them less helpful than they want to be. They recognize that some weaknesses will always remain with them but they see now that these weaknesses, because they have been acknowledged, reflected on, and prayed about, no longer control them as they once did.

Directors become more aware of inhibiting feelings as they arise and can set them aside during direction in order to give full attention to the person with whom they are engaged. As one director said:

> I know that I have an inordinate fear of hearing about evil spirits. As soon as someone starts to tell me about experiencing evil, especially in prayer, I become aware of my panic. Now I turn immediately to God and tell him, "Here we go again. Please help me; don't let my fear get in the way." When I do that, I sense God moving closer and telling me that I'm not being left alone.

Does Supervision End with Graduation?

Directors' need for supervision does not end with the program. The staff encourage graduates to look for a supervisor. Often, however, they are unable to find someone who has both the ability and the time for this enterprise. Because they have experienced the benefits of working with their peers, many graduates initiate or join a group of directors who come together for mutual and continuing help. It is difficult for a director to work for a long time in this sensitive ministry without experienced confidants who can provide support, encouragement, and challenge.

The Supervisor's Attitude to Supervision

Supervisors know the twists and turns of direction relationships. They know how often a director will try to move forward before a directee is ready. They are aware, too, of directors' propensity to hold back, especially when God is very close in the life and prayer of the directee. Supervisors understand the myriad reasons for this back-and-forth aspect of the relationship between directors and directees. They live through the pain and the joy involved in accompanying a director on his or her journey of personal and ministerial development.

Two characteristics of a sound and productive supervisory relationship make the task both attractive and enjoyable: the receptivity and trust of the director and the growing confidence that experience and prayer give to the director. It is heartening to see a director becoming more independent when this quality is accompanied by careful listening to suggestions and reflection on them. When this combination of independence and receptivity characterizes the attitude of the director, the supervisor knows that their work together is accomplishing its purpose.

It is disheartening, on the other hand, to realize after months of work with a director that she or he is still somewhat reserved and defensive. The person can be a capable director, but is not benefiting from supervision as he or she could. Supervisors then must trust that as the person continues in the ministry of direction, she or he will come to more freedom. This greater freedom will eventually enable the director to attend to those inner spaces where growth is still needed.

Chapter 8

The Associate's Year: Encounter and Growth

Introduction

This chapter describes how associates have experienced the associates' program, and Chapter 9 discusses how directees have experienced spiritual direction.

Persons change at different times, in different ways, and in reaction to different influences. This is true of directees. It is also true of those whom directees ask to facilitate their relationship with God. We want to concentrate now on the changes associates say take place in themselves, and what prompts those changes.

The First Faith-Sharing

The first faith-sharing takes place two weeks after the beginning of the program, and often brings about the first of these changes. Associates enter upon the program with hope and desire, glad to be embarking on an enterprise they have looked forward to for months, sometimes for years. As faith-sharing begins, however, their good humor is tinged with nervousness. So far they have only a superficial acquaintance with one another and with the staff. As the weekend gets underway, they become aware that they already have choices to make:

Will I trust what these men and women tell me about their experience of God?

Will I take the risk of disclosing some of my more intimate thoughts and feelings?

An associate named Bev said later: The group was too much for me. I knew that I wasn't free enough to let them inside. It didn't have much to do with them, although I felt critical of everyone. I just couldn't let anyone know what was going on inside me; so I was very selective about what I said. Then I started to feel isolated. I didn't want that, and kept praying that I would become freer. Thank God, that did happen later on.

Bev knew that her reserve would make it hard for associates to come to know her and for directees to be completely at ease with her. Although she did not overcome her inhibitions at that time, she recognized they were there and would have to be dealt with.

The Workshop on Religious Experience

The workshop that follows closely on the initial faith-sharing also calls for face-to-face meetings among the associates and staff. The workshop has a different focus however. During the faith-sharing, the associates and staff try to tell one another something of God's action in their lives, what God has been like for them, what prayer has been like, what persuaded them to become spiritual directors and, finally, what brought them to the Center.

During the second workshop, the associates try to articulate what it was like at the faith sharing meetings to know that people were listening to them and taking seriously what they said. They learn, too, how differently they were heard by different people. They also have opportunities to assess their own ability to hear.

Bewildered at discovering that others in the group heard much more than they did, or heard it more accurately, some begin to question for the first time how well they listen to others. Eric, an associate, said:

> It took me until November to tell Laura, my supervisor, how disconcerted I was by the reflection days. I enjoyed the faith sharing and expected to enjoy the reflection too. On the first day, when people began telling Alex what they heard him say and how it made them feel, I went into shock. I had not heard what they had heard. It was impossible for me to admit that and I became much less vocal with the group than I had been before.

Some associates are dismayed to realize that a painful incident they had related either was not heard at all or was only partly understood. Edith told the group at a February meeting:

> At the September faith-sharing, I thought I was outspoken when I told you I felt betrayed by my family when I was fourteen. I realized that no one had noticed it. None of you reacted to my pain. I got angry and confused and drew a curtain between myself and all of you. I drew the curtain with other people too. It was not until a few weeks ago that I discovered, while trying to help a directee, that my words and my body language often don't match what's going on inside me. What's going on can be excruciating but I don't show it.

As associates reflect on their own experience and listen to the experience of others in the group, they begin to ask themselves:

How well do I listen to those I direct?

Am I sufficiently in touch with my own experience to let it teach me patience and understanding?

What has to change in me so that I can hear what is being said?

Through the days of reflection, then, a process of ministerial growth begins for the associates. Questions have been raised. Often they are personal questions. But all of them point to the possibility that the further development of the associate will enable him or her to become a more effective director.

Beginning to Give Spiritual Direction Again

The transition from talking about spiritual direction to giving it again often brings a kaleidoscopic rush of reactions. Now, after weeks of talk about direction, the die is about to be cast. A surge of adrenaline drives some associates to phone directees in rapid succession so that direction can begin immediately. This may be followed by sensations of lethargy, uncertainty, and even fear. The most experienced associates, women and men who have been giving direction for many years, have said that they begin to wonder not only "What will I say after I've said hello?" but even "How do I say hello?"

A few associates exude a confidence which in reality they do not experience. Around the middle of December, they begin to describe the reactions that haunted them in October, reactions they may have been unable to admit even to themselves. It is often hard to admit confusion and doubt.

Such regression is natural and occurs in the beginning phase of many ventures. The staff, realizing it will not last, view it with equanimity. Associates will not only experience it; they will learn from it.

The first interviews with directees prove excellent restoratives. Directees, though they too may experience some pangs of anxiety, are glad to begin direction, and their eagerness is infectious. Meeting men and women who are looking for direction, and the familiar circumstances of direction itself soon begin to renew the associates' self-assurance.

There are difficult moments, too. Some directees can be aggressive, almost overpowering, in their first interview. Others are shy to the point of being inarticulate. There will always be those who demand to know the history, experience, and credentials of the director. And a few will enter into a process of testing the director that can last for several meetings.

The basic question, of course, is whether directees will finally believe that they can speak frankly and be accepted. When they come to believe this, associates experience in most directees not only personality traits, some agreeable and others less so, but also the sincerity and intensity of the longing for God that have brought them to direction. It then becomes not only possible but easy for the associate to set aside his or her personal doubts and fears and pay attention to the directee's unique search for a more personal God.

A Season of Assimilation

During the Christmas season, a curious phenomenon may occur. Some associates tell us later that when they left for the holidays they did not know whether they would return in January. They had been hearing other associates say that they saw significant growth in the men and women they were directing. This discouraged them. They themselves saw little development in those coming to them for direction. There were other frustrations too. They were weary of talk about religious experience. They questioned the need for so much reflection, especially for written reflections. Writing focusing papers had become tedious. They wondered whether their supervisors understood how hard they were working and what slender results their work could bring. Worst of all, they found that their own prayer was often rushed and unfulfilling. They were weary, discouraged, and bored. They could hardly wait to get away.

Somehow, geographical and emotional distance offered a new perspective. Puzzles began to solve themselves. They missed directees, other associates, even the staff. As weariness abated, so did discouragement. When friends asked them about the program, they found themselves replying enthusiastically. Procedures they had questioned, they now advocated. A sense of interior balance began to assert itself.

One associate, Jan, wondered why she had been so dispirited. When one day at her parents' home she began to muse over a disconcerting direction session, she found herself looking forward to writing a focusing paper about it. Another associate realized as he helped plan a workshop on spiritual direction that he brought to the task far more insight than he had commanded in September.

As the vacation comes to an end, many associates find that returning has begun to take on a cheerful glow. For the most part, a rising sense of achievement characterizes the second term. The difficult moments that occur in all serious endeavors will not be lacking to this one, but a basic confidence asserts itself.

The Mid-Year Review

Before the program begins, each associate receives a calendar of the year's events. Associates often have an immediate reaction to the reviews scheduled for January. Trepidation can arise like a cloud crossing a wintry moon. But January, after all, is far in the future. As the weeks speed by, however, the mid-year reviews begin to loom threateningly on the horizon. Associates wonder: "What are the reviews like, anyway?" They ask themselves how they should begin to prepare for them and what the staff will be looking for.

The staff definitely are looking for something. They want experiential data that show whether the associates recognize and react to religious experience. They also want to know whether associates can help directees to recognize, react to, and talk about that experience. How have the associates usually helped directees to see the relationship between what is happening in their prayer and what is going on in their lives? Can they speak freely to the staff about their strengths and weaknesses and how these traits have affected the quality of their spiritual direction? To address these questions, associates submit a report that describes spiritual growth they have seen in a directee and how they have contributed to it, and growth they themselves have experienced as directors.

Staff members have already received copies of this report, and have considered and discussed it. Some associates look forward to this time with the staff as an opportunity for learning through the discussion of their experience. They may experience some anxiety, but they are also confident that they have developed, and that they will be able to discuss this development.

Others, however, experience disquiet. This uneasiness shows itself in a variety of ways. Minor inconveniences may bring on disproportionate annoyance. They may feel misunderstood by the staff, their supervisor, or other associates. Underlying these reactions is the question: Will they decide I'm a poor spiritual director?

To mitigate this uncertainty, supervisors emphasize the importance of self-discovery, the advantage to associates of recognizing and affirming for themselves both what they are accomplishing and what aspects of their work call for improvement. Associates are reminded that in the review they will have opportunities not only to discuss their weaknesses, but also to point out their strengths.

During the review, nevertheless, the staff are active and not simply acquiescent. The mid-year review is a time not only for encouragement and support, but also for help and challenge. A few examples of the type of discussion that takes place will illustrate this.

During Joe's review, the staff observed that he was not paying enough attention to religious experiences described by the directee. We gave this a good deal of attention, pointing out instances of it in the written report. Finally, exasperated, Joe said: "You think I'm not recognizing religious experience. I recognize it all right. What I've just discovered is that any time a directee starts talking about it, I run like hell." He went on to say that this had not been clear to him until his preparation for the evaluation forced him to face it. He had repeatedly maintained in supervision that he had valid reasons for not paying more attention to religious experience. The directee had to give his attention to childhood traumas first, or had to learn to express his or her anger at past injuries, or required help in learning to pray. Now Joe had discovered for himself what was happening within him, the director, as he made those choices. He was surprised and delighted when the staff expressed satisfaction at his discovery and confidence that it would help him to develop further as a director.

Chris, another associate, showed a marked talent for enabling directees to recognize an experience of God and begin to talk about it. She manifested an even greater capacity, however, for then shifting the directee's focus so quickly away from the experience that the directee had no opportunity to explore it.

Her report illustrated this. Ruth had shared with Chris a prayer experience in which Jesus had impatiently urged her to stop dwelling on her past failures. Ruth remembered as she spoke to Chris that Jesus had also told her that he had accepted the past and that she could stop worrying about it.

Chris: And how did you feel when you sensed Jesus telling you this?

Ruth: Free, as though a great burden had been lifted from my shoulders.

Chris: That must have been a tremendous experience for you. I'm so glad. (a short pause) How did the rest of the week go?

Ruth: Nothing else happened that week—except that every time I prayed it seemed that Jesus was near, very present.

Chris: He has given you a great gift, helping you let go of the past. Now you have an incentive for the future.

Chris and Ruth spent the rest of their time together talking about the positive power of motivation.

We affirmed Chris's ability to help Ruth talk about her religious experience. We also commented on the fact that Ruth recalled more of the experience as she talked to Chris.

We noted too that Chris could have encouraged Ruth to explore her experience even further. This would have enabled Ruth to savor the experience more deeply. We wondered in particular why Chris had not asked what Jesus seemed to be like when he was "impatient" and what Jesus was like when he told Ruth she could let go of the past. We asked Chris what she was experiencing that caused her to inquire so abruptly: "How did the rest of the week go?" When she tried to answer the question, Chris could not remember what she had thought and felt at the time.

One of us asked about Ruth's comment that Jesus had been "near, very present" whenever she prayed after the experience. Chris had given little attention to the statement and did not know whether she had had any feelings about it. She agreed, but reluctantly, that she had not given Ruth a chance to explore her experience thoroughly. We suggested that Chris take time to explore this discovery in reflection and prayer. We also urged her to try with her supervisor's help to discover what feelings had prompted her to minimize the value of Ruth's religious experience. Chris accepted these suggestions, but looked uncertain when she left.

Let us consider the emotional effects of these two interviews. Joe had had a difficult time with religious experience. While preparing for the evaluation he discovered that he was afraid to engage with the experience. Chris too had had difficulty with religious experience. She had not, however, explored the difficulty. The staff had to initiate the exploration, and she was not ready to pursue it during the interview. When Joe left us he felt confident and hopeful. When Chris left she was dejected.

A major factor in the difference between the two outcomes is the sense of personal discovery with which Joe's evaluation ends and Chris's does not. Chris is probably no less capable than Joe. But she and Joe are at different points in their development. Chris has yet to come to her own moment of discovery. To do so, she will need assistance in reflecting on her feelings. When she does reflect on them carefully and repeatedly, she will find herself one day drawn by a directee's religious experience and able to help the person to explore deeply his or her encounter with God.

Few associates are eager to have their work evaluated. Although most believe that their work is acceptable, this belief is usually accompanied by some measure of anxiety that they might not be able to demonstrate their ability. The staff, aware of this anxiety, try to be careful during a review to dwell graphically on the aspects of the associate's direction that demonstrate ability, as well as on those that indicate that further development is necessary.

We have learned, too, that during reviews associates often have an acute ear for criticism and a dull one for approval. This trait can occasion delicate moments in their growth as directors. If they reflect on both their strengths and their mistakes they will tap new resources within themselves and become aware of sound reasons for fresh confidence. If they slip into unqualified self-reproof, they will waste energy that could enable them to continue developing. Often, as we approach the end of a review, we ask: "What have you heard?" If the associate has not heard the approval we have offered, or has heard it dimly, we call his or her attention to the imbalance.

The Mid-Year Faith-Sharing

Shortly after the mid-year review, we return to Seabrook for a second faith-sharing meeting.

The second faith sharing was incorporated into the associates' program soon after the program began. It had its origin in a complaint voiced by associates after they had experienced how busy the year could be.

> We started the year with faith sharing. That was a very good experience. It brought us together with time to relax, pray, talk to one another about God, and be. I thought: This is going to be a good year. That was months ago, and we haven't done anything like it since.

A second faith-sharing meeting in January or February looks far more attractive in November, however, than it does in mid-winter. New England is usually cold and often blustery then, and the prospect of three days at the beach holds little allure.

Faith-sharing itself, seen now as an addition to an already busy schedule, seems low on the collective list of priorities. Why do we have to go? . . . there? . . . now?

> We don't want to seem unreasonable, but did the staff really check the schedule carefully when you decided on this meeting?

> It will be cold at Seabrook in February. And windy. Why can't we just stay here?

> Why do you people want to have faith-sharing now anyway?

As a result of these reactions, the staff has often asked the associates as the time for the meeting approached: "Do you want to go?" Unless the answer has been immediately obvious, time to consider has also been given. So far the associates have always replied, after considering, that they did.

The format of the second faith-sharing is much like that of the first. Individual prayer and communal reflection form the core of the meeting. A staff member opens each session by proposing a question and briefly setting forth a scripture text that can be used as a basis for prayer. About 45 minutes are allotted to individual prayer, and as much time as necessary is given to the participants' description of what happened when they prayed. The dynamic of prayer the staff encourages is again one of receptivity to the communication of God. Usually two sessions take place each day.

The questions are different now. Much new experience has entered the associates' lives since September—experience of God, of ministry, and of one another. Growth and change call for a concentrated time of prayer and reflection. Much has been absorbed; now, as individuals and as a group, they have an opportunity to assimilate it. The questions are attempts to facilitate this assimilation.

The focal questions now are: Where has God brought you since September on your journey of faith? What more do you want to happen before the end of the year? A third question, proposed toward the end of the meeting, is: How can the group help you to get what you want?

A salient feature of the meeting is the opportunity each participant has to describe his or her experience to the whole group. There have been times during the preceding months when most associates talked about their experience to one or two others; and there have been moments—at group life, for instance—when some of us have addressed the whole group. But the mid-winter meeting at Seabrook provides the first opportunity we have had since September to combine the leisure to pray and reflect for appreciable lengths of time with opportunities to tell the whole group what has come to mind in the prayer and reflection.

For some, speaking frankly to the group about their own experience is a simple, straightforward affair. They appreciate their development and want their colleagues to appreciate it with them. For others, speaking candidly is a more complex matter. The associates now know one another better than they did in September. They have usually worked well and companionably together, but the texture of their individual relationships can range all the way from friendship to hostility. They have become accustomed to speaking freely to some, and being more guarded with others. Some have been at the center of every group activity, while others have usually been on the periphery. These differences have affected the inner dynamic of the group, though they have rarely been evident to outsiders.

These differences occur in any group. For the associates, however, they have distinctive consequences related to the basic purpose for which they have come together. Although community and friendships develop, the primary bond among them is the support, encouragement, and challenge they offer to one another as ministers. This bond will be either strengthened or debilitated by the way they relate personally to one another. It cannot go unaffected by the quality of personal relationships or the relationship each person has with the group.

At the end of the year an associate might look back and say something like this:

> At first I tried to relate to everyone equally, trying to spend time with everyone. That didn't make much sense. You have more in common with some people than with others. And I started to run out of time. So I spent my time with those I liked, admired, and could relate to easily, and let the others just be there. When we went away in February for the second faith-sharing, several in the group spoke of the richness and depth of one person I had written off. Then, when he spoke to me, he said he felt deprived because he didn't know me. He admired the way I related to my directees, and had often wanted to speak to me about it, but never had the courage to take the initiative. I was shocked. Well, we talked that day and often afterwards. Now, at the end of the year, I thank God for that February

faith-sharing. The most important discovery for me was how much I had lost by being so closed off. Gil has turned out to be a wonderful friend and even more than a friend. Talking to him and watching him with other people have taught me what ministry is all about.

Mid-Year Ennui

Mid-year ennui often makes its appearance after the mid-winter faith-sharing. Some associates may be asking: What else is new? The program has lost its novelty and they are getting bored.

Yet more signally than the first half, the second half of the program presents associates with distinctive opportunities for ministerial growth. Directees have developed. They are more aware of the forces at work in their inner lives and can go deeper in prayer. Associates are more at ease with the new dimensions of direction to which they were introduced in the fall and can accompany directees to deeper reaches of prayer with firmer assurance. The development that has taken place, however, presents new challenges to a director's attentiveness to directees and to his or her ability to engage with them. When an associate is not alert to these challenges, the directee's vital movements toward deeper growth, which are often unobtrusive, may go unnoticed.

This is the time when associates begin to manifest differences in attitude among themselves toward direction. Some take every opportunity to increase their experience and their understanding of what can happen as they explore in depth with directees; others do capable work, but are not eager for such opportunities. It becomes evident to most associates that after they leave the Center some of them will do as much spiritual direction as they can, while others will do relatively little. Sometimes an associate who shows a less than ardent interest in direction hears a colleague say:

> I find that this ministry is exciting if you give your-
> self unreservedly to it. I hope it can become excit-
> ing for you, too.

Often enough the ennui that makes its appearance around the
time of the mid-winter faith sharing has deeper roots than the
associate imagines. An associate describes his experience to
his supervisor:

> I began to be bored soon after evaluations. You were
> very reasonable about the quality of my spiritual di-
> rection. I didn't realize at the time, though, that I
> was feeling that the program was all over. I began
> to resent having to be supervised and started to lose
> interest in direction. When Jane pushed me at faith-
> sharing about my attitude, I got very angry. Then
> she said: "You act as though you think that you,
> not God, are the one who changes a person's life and
> prayer." That pierced all my defenses.

> Later, when I was praying, I saw for the first time
> some of the options that were available to me as a
> spiritual director. What was even more important,
> though, was the reality Jane reminded me of, that
> it's God who does it, not me. You've been telling us,
> showing us, that all year. What's even harder for me
> is that directees, and God, have been teaching me
> the same thing. Why have I been so slow to get it?

Of all the changes that have to take place in the developing spiritual director, the most unnerving has to do with this
action of God in the directee's life and prayer.

Early in the year we begin to help the associates recognize the tendency there is in all of us to draw away from involvement with a directee's vividly perceived experience of
God. This tendency often shows itself even when the experience is another person's, not our own. Directors, for example,
when they discuss an experience of God, frequently talk at
length about what the person felt, but neglect to ask what

God was like in the experience and what God seemed to be trying to communicate to the person. Yet, if a spiritual director is to help a directee to strengthen the relational aspect of his or her prayer, the director must let himself or herself give full attention to the incursion of Mystery into that prayer.

In the second half of the year this challenge is likely to become more urgent. To meet this challenge associates have to be consciously receptive to God. We are not referring here to the idea of God, or even to God as the associate might perceive God at work in his or her own life, but to God as God makes Godself known in the lives and prayer of directees. If they are not receptive to God as God appears in directees' lives, associates are likely to be satisfied with helping directees come to a new measure of freedom and satisfaction in their lives. In itself this is a valuable achievement, but it may not meet the directee's deepest desire, and it does not of itself satisfy God's desire to be known and engaged with. God not only gives us life and freedom; God seeks to give us God's own self.

Some directors seem never to grasp the significance of God's self-giving for their ministry. Some recognize it but remain wary of treading on the holy ground where God makes that self-giving known. Directors who recognize and respond to God's desire also run less risk of believing that they, not God, are chiefly responsible for a directee's development.

The Final Review

During the mid-year review, the staff give a major part of their attention to the associates' ability to recognize and work with religious experience. In the final review, this focus has changed. Again we take up religious experience; but this time we regard it in light of the interaction of impulses that characterizes the development of a closer relationship with God. We center our inquiry on three questions:

How well can the associate distinguish what is happening within directees that seems to be drawing them into a closer relationship with God?

How well can the associate distinguish what is happening in directees that tends to stop this development?

How does the associate assist directees to let the movements toward development bring about the relationship they and God want?

As associates prepare for these interviews they are usually aware that old anxieties conjured up by the prospect of reviews have not entirely disappeared. Most associates also notice, however, that they are more relaxed and confident than they were in January. They evidence more trust in themselves, in their directees' development, and in God. The staff's primary purpose in these reviews is not to sit in judgment on the quality of associates' work, but to estimate with them the point of development each one has reached. We also hope we can help them to determine how they could develop further.

Some, while reasonably competent, have been more engaged with their personal struggle to overcome anxiety and reserve than they have been with the directees' experience; others are better able to give their attention to directees. Some are more capable than others of engaging with directees' experience of God. It becomes clear in their interviews that some have become enthralled with the largesse, tenderness, and fidelity they have seen God show to directees.

Often associates describe an incident in direction that occasioned significant development in them. It may have occurred in a process of direction that from the first interview was enjoyable and promising. Sometimes it happened in a process that was pedestrian but steadily productive. Surprisingly often, though, it took place in a process that from the beginning the director has found difficult, even irksome. The directee, though he or she professed a desire to relate more

fully to God, seemed to be making no progress toward the fulfillment of that desire, and frequently seemed to be acting at
cross-purposes to it. The director experienced interview after
interview as a trudge through heavy fog without a landmark
in sight. So it went until, in the midst of an interview, the
director looked up one day to find that the fog had abruptly
lifted and that its departure revealed an interaction that was
both intimate and potent occurring between the directee and
God.

It is often the directee who at first seemed least promising in whom the director sees God's desire most poignantly
revealed. An associate says:

> I found him uninteresting. He rambled, talking at
> exorbitant length about the wretched state of the
> world and innumerable difficulties with his work.
> He seemed incapable of settling on any other sub-
> ject. After a few meetings I had just about decided
> to terminate. Then, toward the end of the next
> meeting, he said, "The other day, just when I was
> most discouraged, I had the impression that God
> put his arm around my shoulders." I sat up both
> physically and mentally. I shiver when I realize how
> easily, in my boredom, I could have overlooked that
> remark. When I did pay attention I discovered a
> relationship with God that was no less real for being
> subdued. That was the beginning of an experience
> of direction I'll never forget. I hate to think it's
> over.

The associates who most appreciate what they have accomplished during the year and what has been accomplished
in them, come to the interview with evident anticipation.
They want to discuss their work and to hear staff members'
observations on it. They are not alarmed when missteps are
pointed out or crestfallen when shortcomings appear. While
they acknowledge, sometimes ruefully, that aspects of their
work require further development, they also exhibit firm confi-

dence in the development that has taken place. They look to their future ministry with eagerness and resolve.

Indifference, boredom, even a lack of personal attraction are quickly dissipated by engagement with God and what God is trying to do. They have lived through the arduous plodding that had to be endured when nothing seemed to be happening. And when they have almost lost hope, they have witnessed the plodder soaring on the eagle's wings of God's breaking through.

These individual moments of growth are different for each associate but they become convinced of one unalterable truth. God will do what needs to be done if only the directee perseveres and the director is faithful to the task of facilitating and believing.

Final Faith-Sharing and Graduation

A final faith-sharing meeting precedes graduation. It is a time for clarifying what the year at the Center has been for each one on a ministerial and personal level. Individual gratitude is expressed freely because each person has been a help to the others. It is a time, too, for looking toward the future and expressing hopes, dreams, and expectations. A process has been completed, but has opened up another process in which further growth can take place, and a fuller life can be experienced. A ministry can be offered that is truly for the greater glory and service of God.

Conclusion

Important as the experience of personal growth is for the associate, the director is a director not for his or her own sake but for the sake of those who seek direction. It is the directees' experiences that are of paramount importance in the direction relationship. So we turn in our concluding chapter to their experience of God and prayer. If the efforts of the Center for

Religious Development have been successful, it has been because many who approached it hoping to develop their relationship with God have not been disappointed.

Chapter 9

Key Moments of Growth for the Directee

In this final chapter we turn again to those primarily responsible for this book: the men and women who, seeking God, have shown us the uniqueness of God's relationship with them and of their relationship with God.

To describe their experience, we want to point out and illustrate key moments that often occur in direction. While respecting the uniqueness of each person's experience this procedure will, we hope, convey an accurate impression of how spiritual life can develop in the course of direction.

Reactions to Spiritual Direction Itself

Later in the chapter we want to describe key moments that take place because the person is paying attention to prayer and to God's way with him or her. First, however, we should discuss events that occur simply because the person has begun spiritual direction.

Most of those who have come to the Center for direction have found the time they spent there an unusual experience. Even those who have had spiritual direction before have often found this experience surprising. In the first few meetings with the director much of the time is taken up with getting acquainted and with the discussion of any concern that preoccupies the directee: an illness or death in the family, an important decision to be made, anxiety about a precarious job situation, or any serious threat to the directee's well-being. When the direction has been well begun and the directee's relationship with God is being explored, directees frequently say:

> I'm not used to being listened to with this much attention.

Or

> I'm amazed at how much I can say about what's happened when I've prayed. When I come, I think I have practically nothing to say. But look how much I've said this morning.

The discovery that, when an attentive and interested director is listening, one has a surprising amount to say about what happens when he or she tries to pray is a striking moment. It encourages the directee to take his or her experience of prayer seriously, and to proceed with it. This discovery also gives directees reason to believe that further conversations with the director will continue to increase their awareness of what happens when they pray.

Questioning the Director's Facilitative Approach

Many who come to the Center for direction are surprised by the director's contemplation-oriented, facilitative approach. Although they have heard about this during their initial interview, they often do not realize how much initiative this approach will require of them. A directee might say:

> I have found it helpful to talk to you. You ask some good questions. I wish, though, that you would make more suggestions. My last spiritual director suggested scripture passages that I could use for prayer. She drew up a list of books for me to read, too. They gave me a lot to think about. When I leave here, I don't know where to start.

Comments like these usually lead to a conversation about what the directee wants from direction and how the director believes he or she can be most helpful. Because this conversation can draw for examples on the direction that has already taken place, it is usually more enlightening than were the explanations given before direction began. The directee comes to understand better what he or she can expect from the director and what he must do for himself or she for herself if they are to get what they want from direction.

After this clarification some directees may decide that this is not the kind of direction they are looking for. The better they understand it, the less they want it. If knowing what they do not want leads to a clearer perception of what they do want, the brief experience of direction will have been a valuable one.

Most directees who are at first dismayed at not receiving the guidance they expected will want to talk further about the approach the director is prepared to take. In the ensuing discussion directees may become aware that they have a complex attitude toward exercising freedom in their relationship with God. It is easier to talk about freedom than to exercise it. They may also, however, find the latitude that facilitative direction offers for recognizing God's action wherever it appears as both liberating and exhilarating. Once directees recognize that a director expects nothing from them but a desire for God and for inner freedom, they may decide that this is the kind of assistance they want and need. Their new awareness of the possibility of freedom in their relationship with God can act as a tonic that gives new vigor to their pursuit of that relationship.

Recognizing that Developing One's Relationship with God Involves Patient Striving

The events we will now describe have more to do with the directee's relationship with God than with the process of direction. They occur because the person is trying to develop a closer relationship with God and, in order to do that, is devoting time and attention to communicating with God. These moments probably take place often in the lives of people who are serious about their relationship with God, whether they make use of spiritual direction or not.

Spiritual direction does not make key moments happen. That is God's privilege and the directee's. However, conversation with the director helps the person to take God's invitations seriously rather than dismiss them as fanciful. The director also encourages the directee to talk about the event. This helps the directee to recall what has happened and explore it at greater depth.

These key moments are usually not events that occur once and never occur again. They may happen many times in a person's life, sometimes in similar circumstances, sometimes in circumstances that are very different.

Developing a strong relationship with God is no less demanding than developing a strong relationship with anyone else. This realization often comes as a surprise to people. Many seem to believe that whenever they take the time to pray and "do it right," they will experience a steady sense of peaceful satisfaction. They seem to think that prayer will never be disappointing or involve disturbance.

The first few times a person with these attitudes experiences prayer that is distracted or boring, even touched by unsettling memories and fears, the person often suspects that he or she is using a faulty approach to prayer. "If I were doing it right," the person thinks, "the prayer would be peaceful and interesting."

Directors can help directees with these doubts. They have met them in other directees and, although they do not know what the immediate outcome of the effort will be for any particular person, they do know that the effort to keep praying when the prayer seems unrewarding is important for the development of the person's relationship with God. This conviction can reassure and encourage the directee.

Other sources of encouragement that often appear quite soon after frequent prayer begins are the observations of friends. Directees make comments like this:

> One of my friends said the other day that she's noticed that I seem different. She said I'm more sure of myself.
> Or:
> My wife, Kathy, is amazed that I've gotten so much more patient; she's delighted for me and for herself. I was surprised when she told me that. I honestly hadn't been aware of that much change.

Encountering the Conflict with One's Personal Code

Another key moment occurs when a directee first realizes that responding spontaneously to God can come into conflict with the directee's personal code of acceptable behavior. Since responding to God is associated in our subconscious as well as in our conscious minds with right behavior, this moment will be disconcerting. Then too, our code itself has sources in our subconscious mind. Our subconscious serves us well, but it is not discriminating. What is right for the subconscious is likely to be what was right when we were children. "It is right to be always agreeable to those who are 'good to us,' or with those who 'mean well,'" our subconscious will tell us, or, more frequently, "It is not right to be angry with, or contradict, someone who is good to me." When I find myself angry then with someone who is important to me, whose attitude is benevolent, I may feel guilty. God, however, does not live according to our code of acceptable behavior. Our code may forbid us to feel fear or anger toward such a person.

But God often invites us to let ourselves be aware of our feelings even when we are afraid and angry. Our code may insist that we should never question the policies of those in positions of authority, but God will sometimes urge us to question those policies in the interest of justice. Our code may require us always to resist unfair treatment. But God may ask us to accept an oppressive situation for the sake of a greater good.

Consider a situation in which this last conflict occurs. Roger works as a volunteer in a soup kitchen. He has worked there for six years, but has been thinking recently about giving it up. The new administrator, Ferdy, is efficient but impersonal. He sees Roger's job as serving the guests with as much dispatch as possible. Roger has always considered serving the guests his primary task, but has also spent time in friendly conversation with them as he served them. The guests have reacted well to him and Roger considers both the talking and the serving vital to his work at the kitchen.

As Roger discusses his work with Gordon, his spiritual director, his anger at Ferdy becomes more and more apparent. Finally he becomes so furious that he decides on the spot that quitting the kitchen is the obvious solution. Gordon, after hearing him out and suggesting he not make a decision motivated by anger, urges him to take some time for prayer. He wins a grudging assent.

Two weeks later, Roger returns. After some preliminary conversation, he says:

Roger: Well, to get to the main point, Gordon (His voice trails off and he smiles ruefully).

Gordon: What's that, Roger?

Roger: You remember that the last time I was here I was ready to quit the kitchen?

Gordon: Yes. We talked about that.

Roger: You suggested I let God in on my thinking. I asked him to help. There wasn't much to pray about though. I knew what I had to do. It wouldn't be right to let Ferdy make a doormat of me. So I waited for the right moment to tell Ferdy I was quitting.

Gordon: What happened?

Roger: Something that surprised me! Ferdy blew up at me the other night—again. I didn't say anything right away, but I did speak to him later, as we were leaving. Then, instead of telling him off and quitting, I said: "Look, Ferdy, I'm trying to do my best. I want to keep working here, and I honestly doubt that you'll find anyone much faster, even if they don't talk but just dish up the food."

Gordon: You sound as though you were very much in charge of your feelings.

Roger: That's the surprising thing. I was. And Ferdy seemed surprised too. At any rate, he didn't say any more.

Gordon: What was going on in you, Roger, that made the difference?

Roger: When he lashed out at me, I felt my blood pressure go up, and then later, as I thought about it, out of nowhere, I heard the question . . .

Gordon: The question?

Roger: Yes. As though a voice deep inside myself, asked: "What do you care about most—being right or staying with these people?"

Gordon: Hmm. From deep inside, eh?

Roger: It sounded like what God might say. Not just right, but really right. And I knew too that the battles between Ferdy and myself weren't over. But I'm determined now to keep my eyes on what I want most, and I know God will help me.

Roger's code urges him to resist unfair treatment. Impelled by his hurt and anger, he wants to quit. God's question invites Roger to look beyond his code to his desire to help the guests. If we contemplate God and try to respond to him, God will teach us God's life. If Roger continues to pay attention, God may also show him that prayer will be aimless unless he is willing to be candid with God about his hurt and anger, although candidly expressing his hurt and anger to God would probably also violate his code.

The Need to Measure Up

A person often feels that he or she should not try to associate with God in prayer unless first measuring up to one's own standard of goodness. God may be inviting the person to deeper prayer, but the person's reaction is: "I'm not good enough for that. I have no right to expect God to accept me as a prayerful person." So he or she remains diffident.

He or she thus joins those of us who are convinced that we have to meet a standard before we are entitled to say more to God than "Help me," "I'm sorry," or "I'm grateful." We believe that to say more—to confide to God our half-formed hopes and desires, for example—would be presumptuous. Yet we may want a more confiding relationship with God, and may know that we will not fulfill some of our dearest hopes without such a relationship. This dilemma can last a long time.

Resolution of the Dilemma

Contemplative dialogue with God can gradually resolve this dilemma. Jerry is a priest and a member of a religious congregation. Claire is an associate at the Center when she and Jerry begin spiritual direction. Jerry continues direction with Claire the following year as well. He has been talking to

Claire every week for a few months when the following discussion takes place.

Jerry: I wish I could tell you that I've prayed during the last week, but I haven't.

Claire: Oh? What's been happening?

Jerry: I don't know. I haven't been able to get myself together enough to do it.

Claire: Not gotten yourself together.

Jerry: You know what I mean. I need time and space and tranquillity to pray. There hasn't been much of any of them. (He pauses.) Especially tranquillity.

Claire: I know what that is like for me. Can you tell me what it's been like for you? Not enough tranquillity.

Jerry: Have you ever sat, trying to pray, with one irrelevant thought after another trooping through your mind? Things to be done, things you wish you could do but can't, things you wish you had done while you could? None of them having anything to do with God or with anything else that is important to you.

Claire: Yes, I have. Often.

Jerry: What do you do when that happens?

Claire: Different things. A lot depends on what I want at the time. When I'm serious about being with God and communicating with him, I often try to recall what he has seemed like recently.

Jerry: What God has seemed like recently. What sort of thing would you recall?

Claire: Jerry, I'm willing to talk about that. But what do you think? Would it be more helpful if we talked about your own experience? For instance, has anything reminded you of God in the last few days?

Jerry thinks and then says:

I was reading a section of Matthew's gospel the other day as part of my preparation for a homily, and came upon "Be perfect, as your heavenly Father is perfect." I thought to myself: How impossible that is!

Claire: How impossible.

Jerry: How can anyone ever be that perfect? (He pauses and spends a minute in deep thought.)
How could you ever make it?

Claire: You look pensive. How does the thought make you feel?

Jerry: I might feel hopeless if I let myself think about it much.

Claire: Let's look for a moment. Do you mind?

Jerry: What is there to look at?

Claire: Well, the sentence, "Be perfect, as your heavenly Father is perfect" says something to you. What does it say?

Jerry: It says—well, I know what it's supposed to say. What it says to me is that I don't measure up.

Claire: That you don't measure up.

Jerry: That I'm not measuring up. That I'll never measure up.

Claire: You're saying that with a lot of feeling.

Jerry: Why don't I? We've talked about my gifts. I've been given a lot. I'm grateful, though I probably should be more grateful. But with all those gifts I should be a lot better than I am. I should be less egocentric, more generous. I should be more prayerful. My life should be more consistent.
As I'm talking, I feel inconsequential. I'm aware it's Holy Thursday, and that the day probably has something to do with my mood. Tonight we'll recall the priesthood of Jesus, and I'll celebrate my own priesthood. I'll be glad to do that. I'm happy to be a priest. There's nothing else I would want to be. But I can't help feeling inconsequential, especially today. Here I

am a priest, and as I prepare to celebrate Jesus's priesthood I'm acutely aware that I'm not measuring up to what I should be.

Jerry's Concern

We can interrupt Jerry's conversation with Claire to reflect on what has happened between them. The reader will probably agree that Jerry appears to be a sincere, honest man. His alertness to his reactions as he contemplates the gospel and reflects on his life indicates that he has benefited from his spiritual direction with Claire. It may seem to the reader that a careful reading of the passage from Matthew and a knowledgeable interpretation of it would eliminate his consternation. However, he has told Claire, "I know what it's supposed to say." It is not the gospel passage itself, but the sense of "not measuring up" that concerns him.

Notice that Jerry has for the last week been unable to give much attention to personal, relational prayer. He attributes this at first to his lack of "time and space and tranquillity." Only when he recalls the "Be perfect" passage does he mention his conviction that he "does not measure up." Would he have mentioned it or even been fully aware of it if Claire had been willing to discuss his lack of time and space as scheduling issues? Probably not. While direction sessions center on lack of time and space, the directee may experience little or no incentive to explore his deeper experience. Direction then can become an endless search for enough time and space to pay attention to the God to whom, deep in his heart, the directee does not yet want to pay attention.

The New Dimension

When Claire asks Jerry whether he recalls anything that has recently reminded him of God, she is, of course, being "directive." She is introducing a new dimension into the conversation, a dimension that Jerry is free to consider or dismiss. If he does consider it, the conversation can proceed to a new level. It can become concerned with why Jerry is not giving time to prayer, rather than with what is going on between Jerry and God.

A person who believes that he does not measure up could derive this attitude from contemplation of the Other. Jerry, as his contemplation of God developed in prayer, could have become convinced that God is so profoundly good that his own attempts at goodness must always be paltry in comparison. Jerry's conviction that he does not measure up does not seem to result, however, from his contemplation of God. Contemplation encourages further attention to God. Jerry's preoccupation with not measuring up militates against his paying attention to God.

Notice how often Jerry uses the word "should" when he describes his attitude. "I should be a lot better than I am," "I should be more generous," "I should be more prayerful." Strong emphasis on what he should be or should do focuses his attention on himself. As long as Jerry concentrates on what he should be and do, he can focus little attention on God. The saying of Jesus that Jerry has quoted might in other circumstances have drawn Jerry's attention to God and what God is like. Here it does not. Instead he worries the bone of his own inadequacy.

In his self-criticism, Jerry resembles a man trying to find the key to a lock. He has tried several, and none of them works. But this does not shake his conviction that somewhere there is a key that will work. If he can find it, he believes, he will have the solution that will enable him to be the person he should be. His concentration is likely to increase until he either finds the key or abandons the attempt.

The Conversation Continues

We now take up again his conversation with Claire. Jerry has just said: "I'm acutely aware that I'm not measuring up to what I should be."

Claire: You're not measuring up to what you should be. You seem to know what you should be. What tells you that?

Jerry: (After a pause) That's a surprising question. What tells me? I suppose God does. I'm pretty aware of that today. In Jesus God lets me see what I should be.

Claire: God lets you see in Jesus what you should be.

Jerry: Yes. In the way Jesus is at the Last Supper and during the Passion I see what God expects of me: the integrity, the whole-heartedness, the courage, the whole full-blooded relationship with the Father.

Claire: God is showing you all those qualities and letting you know that this is what you should be.

Jerry: Yes. That's it.

Claire: Is God letting you know anything else?

Jerry: The importance of self-sacrifice.

Claire: Anything about what God is doing for you?

Jerry: Well, sure. He is redeeming me.

Claire: Redeeming you.

Jerry: Freeing me, caring for me. Loving me.

Claire: Freeing you, caring for you, loving you.

Jerry: Yes. All of those.
(He pauses for a few minutes.)
That's a lot to say. It is a whole lot to say.

Claire: How does it make you feel?

Jerry: As though it's too much. It's too much to do for anyone.

Claire: Mm.

Jerry: This is a whole different tack, isn't it?

Claire: Different from what we've been talking about. How does it make you feel?

Jerry: (Pause) Maybe overwhelmed. I want to get away from it.

Claire: Anything else?

Jerry: Maybe—drawn.

A Choice Between Introspection and Relational Prayer

At this point in the conversation, Jerry has arrived at a crossroads. Seeing Jesus as the model against whom he should measure the quality of his life still leaves him preoccupied with measuring up. If he continues on this road, his attitude will be no less introspective, concentrated on observation and analysis of himself. Nor is it more likely to lead him to the interaction of personal prayer. However, the road of continuing introspection is not the only road open to Jerry. He can also begin to contemplate Jesus taking an interest in him, caring for him, loving him. He can, instead of focusing on his inadequacy, begin to center his attention on God's attitudes toward him and on Jesus's initiatives on his behalf. We say "can." He will probably have to contend—for months or years—with a wiry tendency to be preoccupied with not measuring up. The new road that has opened before him is not likely to be straight and smooth. It may have detours and be strewn with boulders. But it is likely to be passable.

A significant moment has occurred in Jerry's relationship with Jesus. He has begun to see Jesus freeing him, caring for him, loving him. What he has seen has affected him on the level of feeling. Jerry feels almost overwhelmed. He is attracted, yet he wants to get away. The new road opening up to him is the ability to let himself be drawn toward contemplating God and Jesus, the ability to pay attention to them and what they are doing.

Growth in Contemplative Prayer

Jerry continues spiritual direction for several more months through the summer and fall. Much of his prayer focuses on paying attention to Jesus who has now taken on a clearer personality for Jerry. Gospel passages seem alive with new discoveries, as Jesus reveals the reality of his own joys, anger, happiness, loneliness, rejection. Jerry has been surprised by his tears when he contemplates Jesus being rejected by his own people. He has empathized with Jesus' physical fatigue and hunger. He has argued with Jesus in prayer and disagreed with some of Jesus' decisions. Prayer is a giant clipper under full sail cutting easily through the sea. There have been times of distraction, times when he has not wanted to pray and has not. Jerry has had bouts of boredom to contend with too. But on the whole he has moved steadily ahead and is pleased with prayer and with Jesus revealing himself so abundantly.

Jerry looks forward to Christmas. He anticipates that Jesus will come even closer during those days. As Advent unfolds, he tells Claire that he senses urgency and eagerness in himself as he prays over scripture passages that call on the Lord to come and not delay. He even feels himself holding his arms out expectantly, waiting to embrace the infant. When he comes to see Claire a few days after Christmas, however, a black cloud has enveloped him. Christmas was one of the worst days he can remember. He tells Claire:

Jerry: I had been praying for about half an hour. I was just watching, watching Mary hold the infant and then give him to Joseph. I said to Mary: "Let me hold him too." But she seemed to say "No. The child is not for you."

(Jerry is silent and his face is tight with pain.)

Claire: Not for you . . . oh, how painful.

Jerry: I felt as though I had walked into a concrete wall. I haven't really prayed since.

Claire: You were hurt, really hurt, and you haven't prayed at all since then. You must feel very discouraged.

Jerry: I do. I can't go back to that scene. I have tried a couple of times, but all I seem to hear is a voice saying in the midst of blackness "Too easy. It's too easy." And I don't know what that means.

Eventually Claire helped Jerry to describe the voice more clearly. It had not been scolding, but matter of fact. Still, Jerry remained fearful of the darkness and the voice. Claire suggested that Jerry might approach the Jesus of the Gospels, the person he had come to know, with whom he felt at home. He was not eager but said he would try. When he returned two weeks later, he started without preamble.

Jerry: These last two weeks have been difficult. It took a lot of effort to speak to Jesus. Finally I did. I told him that I was willing to hear that voice again but that I needed him to be with me.

Claire: It was hard, but you managed to do that?

Jerry: Yes, but for several days nothing happened.

Claire: And then?

Jerry: The only way I can explain it is that I had a sudden flash of Jesus and he seemed both close and disappointed.

Claire: Close and disappointed at the same time. Could you say more?

Jerry: It happened so quickly that I had no time to react. As I felt his disappointment, I thought I heard him say, quietly and very carefully: "You'd feel safe with me as an infant, wouldn't you? Then you'd never have to be concerned with measuring up. You'd never have to work that through. It's too easy."

Claire: Wow . . . and it was Jesus saying that to you, that it's too easy?

Jerry: Right. I got angry and said to him: "So it *is* a problem for you."

Claire: You sound aggressive, Jerry. How was Jesus with that?

Jerry: He smiled and said that it wasn't a problem for him but it was for me.

Claire: Measuring up? Your problem, but not his?

Jerry: Exactly. I can't remember the sequence of events after that. At some point, I experienced him saying that he had told me everything he could, but that I didn't believe him. I continued to feel angry. But then I heard myself saying: "If I let go of that, then I have no excuse."

Claire: No excuse? No excuse for what, Jerry?

Jerry: For letting him come closer, as close as he wants to . . .

Let us pause to summarize and reflect on what we have observed. Initially Jerry's concern with not measuring up kept him centered on himself and unable to pray. With Claire's help he began to make choices that enabled him to pass beyond his preoccupation with "should" and contemplate Jesus.

Jesus revealed himself generously. As a result, Jerry was able to cry with Jesus and argue with him. His fears about not measuring up had been put to rest. They had not, however, been resolved. Then, in the midst of ongoing and expectant prayer, Jerry suddenly experienced what seemed strong rejection and was plunged into darkness and confusion. Instead of continuing to look at the darkness and confusion, Jerry, at Claire's suggestion, turned again to the Jesus he had come to know and trust. Neither Claire nor Jerry could know what God was trying to accomplish. They could trust, however, that God knew. And they could believe that if Jerry kept his attention on Jesus, this would give God an opportunity to act.

Who, after all, would argue with a directee who is moved in his prayer to hold the infant Jesus? Only Jesus himself. And it is Jesus himself who challenges Jerry to look at and to recognize that he is using his fear of not measuring up to avoid a deeper intimacy with Jesus.

Overcoming the Fear of Intimacy with Jesus

After talking with Claire, Jerry resolves to try to let Jesus continue to speak to him. During their next meeting, he tells her:

Jerry: I couldn't do it at first, but after several attempts I began to explore what I meant. You remember; when I said if I gave up my fear of not measuring up, I would have no excuse for not letting Jesus come as close as he wanted to come.

Claire: You had to work at persevering with that.

Jerry: Yes, because I was honestly bewildered by what I said.

Claire: It sounds as though you spent a lot of time and energy trying to figure it out.

Jerry: (Laughing) Exactly! And then I just said to Jesus: "You better tell me because I really don't know and you seem to."

Claire: Mm.

Jerry: It was extraordinary! In a flash, I was back with Mary and she was holding the baby for me to take.

Claire: Wow! Before she had refused, and now she offers the child to you.

Jerry: I took him, and held him. I stayed that way in prayer for a long time, and then without even thinking about it, I gave the child back to Mary and told her that I had to go.

Claire: You had to go? How were you feeling then? Do you remember?

Jerry: Calm and deliberate. My eyes were closed but I felt as though I were moving across a wide space and that somewhere the real Jesus was waiting for me.

Claire: The real Jesus—how was that?

Jerry: Oh, it wasn't that the child wasn't real, but more as though if I wanted to be real I had to do it by relating to the adult Jesus.

Jerry has come face-to-face with a discovery familiar to those who pursue at length a conscious relationship with Jesus. At some point in the relationship Jesus will invite them to closer intimacy with him. The invitation is seldom given only once; it comes repeatedly. Nor is the shape the intimacy takes always the same. The invitation often elicits multiple reactions. Often the person invited desires closer intimacy, yet shrinks from it. We fear what it may cost to give ourselves with less restraint. It is a strange phenomenon in the relationship that we seldom seem to wonder what it is that Jesus wants to share with us. Instead, we concentrate on what it is we may be called upon to give. As Jerry continues his association with Jesus, he will find many ways to avoid responding to Jesus's invitations. He can also continue to look at Jesus and allow Jesus to reveal himself to him. In this continuing revelation of Jesus, Jerry will find the strength and attraction that will draw him toward closer intimacy.

An Invitation to Companionship

Intimacy with Jesus is a precious fulfillment of the heart's desire for any directee. It does not represent, however, the ultimate fulfillment of spiritual life. There is more to the developing relationship than closeness. Jerry and God have formed solid ground for communication with one another, but life does not stop there.

The following conversation with Claire now takes place.

Jerry: My prayer seemed quite different to me this week. Not so much good or bad, but different . . .

Claire: Can you tell me something about it?

Jerry: I was praying with Mark 6, the passage about the feeding of the multitude. It was attractive to me. After I'd been praying for awhile, I found myself standing at the edge of the crowd, listening.

Claire: You were attracted and listening, but not quite a part of the group?

Jerry: Yes. And then I sensed that Jesus was looking at me, beckoning me closer to him.

Claire: What did he seem like when he was beckoning?

Jerry: That was unusual (pause). He seemed impatient, almost peremptory, as though he thought I was not being serious.

Claire: As though he thought you were not being serious?

Jerry: I felt confused. I guess alarmed would be a better word. Yes, alarmed rather than confused.

Claire: So Jesus gave you the impression that he thought you were not being serious and that alarmed you?

Jerry (After a long pause): No, that's strange. What alarmed me was that he wanted me to get closer.

Jerry continued to use the same passage for prayer and kept trying to look more closely at what Jesus was doing. He also tried to tell Jesus about his reactions. Jesus seemed to be telling him that he cared about these people and wanted Jerry to care about them too. During his next visit with Claire, Jerry was able to say more:

Jerry: In some ways I believe I'm clearer about what's going on in my prayer, but in other ways I'm not.

Claire: What would be most helpful for us to look at first?

Jerry: Jesus. The more I kept my attention on him, the clearer he seemed to be.

Claire nods and listens.

Jerry: You know, he really had been serious when he invited the apostles to go off and be alone with him. But when he saw the crowd waiting for him he knew he couldn't disappoint them. So he scuttled his own plans to take care of them.

Claire: They were needy and they were important to him.

Jerry: Right. He was willing to disappoint the apostles. I got a strong sense that he expected them to understand and go along with him.

Jerry sits quietly, but nods his head with increasing vehemence. Then he smiles.

Claire: That's saying something important to you.

Jerry: I was glad I was in my room. I said out loud to Jesus that I wouldn't have liked that if I had been one of the apostles.

Claire: What happened?

Jerry: Jesus said they didn't like it either. Then he shrugged his shoulders and said kind of wryly, "Too bad." It made me laugh and he laughed too.

Claire: And then?

Jerry (very seriously): I was standing at a little distance from Jesus. I felt that He was telling me again to come closer.

As Claire and Jerry continued to talk, it became clear that the conversation with Jesus had then dwindled away. He remembered few details. He did recall, however, that he had found himself unable to approach Jesus. Finally he had finished the prayer by telling Jesus he was confused and resentful but did not know why. He told Claire ruefully that maybe he did not want to move closer. His resentment surprised him. He realized that he would have to return to the scene because he and Jesus were not finished with one another.

Jerry returns in a few weeks, quite calm and peaceful, yet very serious.

Jerry: A great deal has gone on in prayer and I want to tell you as much as I can about it.

Claire: Good, Jerry. How would you want to start?

Jerry: I kept trying to talk to Jesus about my resentment. Then I felt anger, then fear. Through it all, I experienced Jesus still motioning to me to come. When I was finally able to say I was afraid Jesus said: "Look, I want you to stand beside me and see what I see. I want you to look at all those hungry people and I want you to care about them as I do." I experienced a remarkable change. Up to that time my major desire was simply to see God, to see Jesus, so that something could happen between us. When I let myself stand with him, side by side, it was as though a new world was opening before me. I was moved by the needs of all those people, and I wanted to care for them as Jesus did. I felt as though he was telling me that from now on, he wanted me to walk with him, not behind him. He said it would be hard. And then he said he needed me, that he couldn't do it alone.

Claire: Jerry, how did all that make you feel?

Jerry: Frightened, humble.

Claire: Anything else?

Jerry: Proud, chosen . . .

A Relationship of Mutual Trust

It is crucial to our understanding of the new development in Jerry's relationship with Jesus that we give close attention to one salient fact. Jesus does not issue a particular mandate: "Go to Brazil and minister to my poor," or "Study law and take up a ministry to prisoners." Jerry may well opt for a new ministry either now or later, but choosing a new ministry is not the point of this conversation. Throughout our description, Jerry's prayer has been oriented toward Jesus and himself. It has changed Jerry, and opened him to intimacy with Jesus, with God. Now Jesus is asking Jerry not simply to associate with him. He is encouraging Jerry to stand beside him and to become involved with what is important to Jesus: the multitudes needing to be fed physically, and needing also to be nourished by the richness of the Word of God. This is essentially a call to companionship, an invitation to be with Jesus, to care about those he cares about, and to work with Jesus.

A shift like this can take place only when a person is able both to trust Jesus and allow Jesus to trust him. What do we mean by "able to allow Jesus to trust him?" Often when we pray we find ourselves asking for an increase of trust in God. We want to believe that God will bring us and those we love through any crisis. We seldom contemplate the trust at the other end of the relationship. Jesus relied on his apostles. He trusted them to share in his responsibility. Although the Gospels tell us that in particular instances they failed him, he never withdrew the confidence he had placed in them.

When a person can both trust Jesus and allow Jesus to trust him or her, prayer no longer centers on what the person needs. It begins to centers on Jesus's desires for his people. The person desires to give as Jesus gives. He or she will always need, and will be no less likely to address his or her needs to God. But there is a new incentive at the core of the person's relationship with God: the person wants to stand at the side of Jesus and do whatever can be done to satisfy Jesus' longing to help the multitude.

What the person will give and how the person will minister is most often left to the person's choice. The choices, however, are influenced by the new incentive. Some will choose to adopt a new ministry; others will decide to continue the life and ministry they have already chosen, instilling into them new optimism, courage, hope, and enthusiasm.

So we are not speaking here of great ministerial ventures for the Lord. Fantasies that have us trekking through the jungles of Borneo or across the frozen tundras of the North when we have a wife and four children to support are helium-filled balloons that excite us for the moment, but they soon shoot up into the sky and disappear. Most of us will continue our routine of daily living as secretaries, administrators, teachers, or homemakers. But the call to companionship with Jesus demands that we see "the multitudes" within our reach. We begin to balance self-centeredness by picking up the burden of becoming more caring people.

Conclusion

Many hours of discussion, reflection, and experience have led us to describe spiritual direction in these chapters both as a way of life and as mystery.

It is a way of life for the directee because it deals with relationship; relationship, rather than being a series of events, is a continuing interaction with another. Each relationship with God is unique, although every relationship shares the common characteristic of invitation. From the very beginning of the relationship, God's unyielding love continually invites, beckons, and pursues. God's activity is never-ending and God's inventiveness is boundless. God needs to be inventive since we are often so slow to notice God's attempts to capture our attention.

Once we do pay attention, we discover that neither the invitations nor our answers are sterile or devoid of feeling. After the invitation come reaction and response. The reaction may be fear, joy, eagerness, faint-heartedness, or any other of the numerous members of the great family of feelings. The response strengthens or diminishes the relationship. We find out, though, that whatever the response is, the relationship continues. It is, in fact, the substance of life. Either we allow God to reveal more and more to us or we develop an attitude that makes it difficult for God to penetrate our defenses. God's initiative can never be exhausted, but that initiative waits for its fulfillment upon the directee's stance of acceptance or rejection of God's invitation.

Gladly we see in the ministry of spiritual direction that the majority of those we have walked with have come to recognize and trust God's action in their lives.

The director is a privileged witness to God's activity as it unfolds in another's life and the director cannot help but be affected by the growth and change taking place in a person who is interacting with God. As the director trusts more and more in God's activity, he or she experiences less compulsion to tell the directee what the directee should think. Instead, a director grows in freedom and is able to encourage the directee to continually return to God, the source of the invitation and experience.

The director's intuitive and analytical powers give way to the major movement that exists between God and the person. The role of the spiritual director is not diminished, but it is clarified. The responsibility for movement is focused where it belongs, between God and the directee.

The director is likely to find, too, that commitment to this ministry also brings a deepening commitment to one's own personal growth. We become more and more conscious of the privilege that is ours and we watch, at times with bated breath, as we see firsthand how unflagging God's energy is. God's tenacious pursuit unfolds before us and is indelibly printed in our minds and in our hearts. We notice other things too. We notice how often God pauses, even seems to withdraw slightly, so that directees are never overwhelmed by God's desire for friendship. We see that God cares deeply and we see that God adjusts to our rhythm, to our pace, to our needs. Our own trust, love, courage, and desire are enkindled and we too grow stronger and steadier in our personal search for a living relationship with God.

In this way of life, both the director and the directee come to know that the most exciting element of spiritual direction is experiencing God as God searches out the most potent ways in which to entice, draw, challenge, and love the other into relationship.

Spiritual Direction as Mystery

Spiritual direction will always include Mystery because God is mystery and will not be categorized. There are some directors, however, who approach this ministry as a theoretical, educative process. They look for techniques and skills that they can use to produce specific results. Their questions tend to emphasize the role of the spiritual director as one who can achieve certain consequences if the correct tools are used.

What method can you use, they ask, to get directees to change their sense of God? How do you get directees to move from self-centered prayer based on problems? Such questions are understandable and often serve a useful purpose. However, they focus more on what the director must do and less on the Mystery of God interacting with each individual person.

Spiritual direction, from beginning to end, is permeated with mystery. The questions revolving around an appreciation of this fact are different: By what new paths is God's love seeking this person? How can I be alert to what God seems to be doing in the person's life?

God's life is both fact and Mystery. But God's love is so rooted in mystery that we can never hope to divide and subdivide either fact or mystery into steps that can be studied and therefore eventually predicted. God's love simply is. We are called upon, as directors, to point to and witness to the reality of that mystery. It is a mystery that is available to us and fathomless at the same time.

It is mystery because it invites us to complete dependence on God and invites us also to complete freedom. It is mystery because while it teaches us that God is everything, it also teaches us to appreciate our own individual worth and personal value as people who make a difference to life. It is mystery because it calls us to give up everything and, at the same time, to possess the invaluable riches of relationship with God. And finally, it is mystery because we come to understand that God will not coerce us into loving or following God.

God waits with infinite patience, unswerving love, and a belief in us that is sometimes terrifying in its intensity. As long as we work with others in the ministry of spiritual direction we are faced with God's surprises. God approaches each person differently and spiritual directors who accept this fact and are excited by it will find themselves better able to work with God's action. There is no way we can guess what God is likely to do. There are no standard questions because there are no standard answers. But if we are content to accept God's Mystery, then God will enable us to help our directees see God more clearly and to trust God's activity more surely. As this happens, we can rest in the certainty that we have cooperated with God's action. We have enabled another to see the fire and witness to its reality. The fire is the hunger and thirst God has for us.

We see the directee being warmed at God's fire and offering the live coals of his or her love to God in return.

"I have come to set fire to the earth, and how I wish it were already kindled."